Trust & Let Go

Play Better Golf Without Consciously Changing Your Swing

Peter Ballingall

Contents

Acknowledgements

My thanks to **Ian & Mhairi Walker** and **Colin Bothway** who created the **Barnham Broom Golf & Country Club** in **Norfolk,** and who took the risk of engaging me as the first Professional & Director of Golf. Barnham Broom gave me the platform on which to run my golf school business that was to become the most popular and successful Golf School in the U.K. for over twenty years.

Thanks to **Michael Harris**, Editor of **GOLF MONTHLY,** for allowing me to reproduce these selected articles that appeared in this great magazine.

Thanks also to **Patrick, Tarn, Kim, Reymond, Edunjobi** and all the staff at **Publishing Push** for their help, professionalism (and extreme patience with me) in producing this book.

To **Malcolm Campbell**, who, in so many ways, increased my profile in the golfing world.

Thanks also to the hundreds of people, far too numerous to mention, who returned to my school many times and who recommended me to their friends. It is true to say that when clients return, they become friends. Many of them, indeed, did became my friends.

Thanks to, **Helene,** my wife, for putting up with this grumpy old man at home and for being my most loyal supporter in my work.

Testimonials

"I fondly remember in the 1980's, as a young PGA Pro, reading articles written by Peter Ballingall.
They were very different from the standard technical swing information so widely available.
Little did I realize at the time how far ahead Peter was with this information.
He was, and is, a visionary.
His articles written back then have absolutely stood the test of time, and by reading the content you will open up to previously hidden areas of your true potential.
Let Peter take you on that voyage of discovery.
You are in very safe hands."

— KARL MORRIS
Founder of THE MIND FACTOR
info@themindfactor.com

"Peter Ballingall is the best golf coach I have ever had.
His seemingly simple concepts and messages are incredibly effective.
Previously I concentrated on my backswing. Peter coached me to trust my swing and focus on making a world class finish. That very season I achieved my golfing ambition of a single figure handicap – age 68!
Needless to say, I have returned for more coaching sessions and am delighted that he has committed his wisdom to a book".

— HELEN STONE OBE

"I met Peter Ballingall for the first time in the spring of 86.

I was a lowly paid assistant pro but drove three hours to see him, such was his reputation.

I was so impressed by his generosity of time and genuine passion to help me.

We talked and, after an hour or so, went out to hit some balls and putts.

My life changed that day!

What I was hearing was opening a door to real improvement without recourse to the usual technical mumbo jumbo but, instead, a holistic way of looking at athletic movement and performance.

I would visit Peter multiple times and I played my life's best and easiest golf.

Peter wrote in his column how I would become a stalwart on The European Tour and I enjoyed my competitive career, though it wasn't as glittering as I had hoped.

I am now a golf coach in Sweden and the principles I learnt from Mr. Ballingall are the foundations of my coaching. I doubt he realizes what an enormous influence he has been on my life.

I hope that you who embrace the wisdom in this book will, like me, play and appreciate this wonderful game on a higher level."

— MARK DEWDNEY
PGA Professional (Sweden)
info@mdgolf.se

Introduction

Most golf instruction books are too long.

The reader is obliged to begin on page 1 and plough through several hundred pages to reach the end.

They contain so much information, the author wanting to give you everything, so that the mind of the poor reader is in 'overload,' and quite unable to assimilate all the detail contained.

This book is different. It contains a compilation of highly acclaimed articles that previously appeared in GOLF MONTHLY – Europe's best-selling golf magazine in the '80s (possibly still today).

The articles are narratives about real people of all levels of experience who attended The Peter Ballingall Golf School during that period, seeking to progress their game.

The reader is not dragged through a series of 'how to' and 'what not to' when playing the game because, I repeat, the articles are true stories of people who made their discoveries, and who made much progress without consciously changing their swing.

> **Everyone** can play better golf naturally
> Everyone **can** play better golf naturally
> Everyone can **play better golf** naturally
> Everyone can play better golf **naturally**

This compilation makes for great bed-time reading that teaches you all you need to know in a subliminal way: no 'heavy instruction'!

You will discover things like:

- The only purpose of the golf swing.
- All golfers are 'unique' – so, too, are their swings
- Everything depends on the Set Up. The Set Up at address determines what happens next
- Problem Solving. The ball is the best instructor. That what it does, once collected by the face, teaches you what you did.
- Mind Management and how to control one's thinking
  ... and much more.

Enjoy.

About the Author

Everyone needs a bit of luck at some point in their lives, whether that is to be in the right place at the right time, or to meet a person who might change one's life.

Such strokes of luck, I believe, are 'accidents made on purpose,' brought about by some star in the universe!!

I got lucky three times in the earliest stages of my career in golf.

In 1969 I met JOHN JACOBS. To be honest I didn't know then who he was, but he offered me a job as Manager of his Golf Centre in Newcastle upon Tyne that was not doing well. I had a young family and I needed a job. I had no special talents but I was a 'people person,' with a big heart and a desire to do well. I didn't let him down and over my seven years of being there I completely turned around the fortunes of his company.

Very quickly I came to realize just how famous he was as a Professional Golfer and as a Teacher of the game; without doubt the greatest teacher ever.

During his frequent visits to the Centre I appeared forever in his shadow, listening to him teach his students. The simplicity of his advice always seemed to lead to immediate improvement.

He never had a 'one swing fits all' philosophy and he taught nothing but the 'ball-flight laws' that you, the reader, will understand clearly in this book.

When I began teaching myself I, too, became successful as I followed his example.

When the time came for me to leave, his fame and reputation opened other doors for me in my career that followed.

R.I.P. John. I thank you.

My next piece of luck came from meeting and becoming friends with JENNY LEE SMITH. She was a golfer of exceptional talent, both as an amateur and as a professional.

On a return from the U.S.A she brought with her a book entitled THE INNER GAME OF GOLF by Timothy Gallwey. "This is a must read" Jenny told me. "It has transformed my thinking when playing the game in high-stress tournaments".

I read it and was amazed to discover simple ways of controlling the demon that sits there at the front of our golfing minds. It established an entirely new route that I was going to take, in the way I would teach my clients in the future.

With John Jacobs in my heart and The Inner Game in my head there was no way that I couldn't possibly succeed.

My third piece of luck was in meeting MALCOLM CAMPBELL, the editor of GOLF MONTHLY in the 80's; Europe's best-selling quality golf magazine at the time and, possibly still, today.

How we met is another story but we spent an enjoyable weekend at Barnham Broom playing and talking golf. This most gregarious of people has an amazing command of the English language so that when he writes, the reader is totally consumed and entertained.

He invited me to write six articles for his magazine! Me? My name was to be in print? Wow!! Had I arrived?

Of course, after his departure, I locked myself away and wrote those six articles. They were not going to be like the normal 'boring' advice usually given in instruction articles. They were going to be narratives about real people of all levels of experience, who had attended my Golf School, who sought a release from their own demons and who were seeking to improve.

I waited impatiently for the 'first edition' to be printed that, hopefully, would seal my fate for the future.

After the third article had been published Malcolm called me on the phone to tell me that the feedback from his readers had been fantastic and so could I keep writing in the months ahead?

The result of this was that it led to a dramatic increase in the numbers of clients attending my Golf School, and they came from every golfing nation on the planet!

Without this exposure it would not have been possible.

Furthermore, in the 90s, it was Malcolm who recommended me to Dorling Kindersley, the publishers, to produce their book, LEARN GOLF IN A WEEKEND, that went on to sell half a million copies worldwide in nine languages.

Yes, I was very lucky to encounter these three very special people. Each one in their own way gave me the knowledge, opportunity and exposure to be a different kind of teacher to the rest – and a successful one too!

Doing What Comes Naturally

April 1983

What is it that makes golf one of the most difficult games to master? Indeed, who could ever claim to have mastered it?
And why is it that, in spite of all the golf books written, and the instructional articles which appear in magazines, and are read by millions all over the world, the standard of golf is so poor?

Surely the experts and authors of these articles can't *all* be wrong. Yet over 80% of all the golfers in the world have either not yet qualified for a handicap, or possess a handicap of over 18. This means that, if you are 18 handicap you rank in the top 20% in the world but still make a mistake which costs you a shot at EVERY hole. Your colleagues at the club are considered 'semi-pro' and yet even they, *at every other hole*, on average, make a costly mistake.

It seems to me that those statistics account for the reason why golf is considered to be a very complicated and difficult game. Some golf teachers have compounded this thinking by analysing the "swing" to the nth degree, so that there are now 146 movements to make in the backswing, and 183 on the downswing. Perhaps I exaggerate! (perhaps others would argue that there are even more!!! Horrors!).

The point I want to make is that the golf swing takes approximately two seconds to complete, from start to finish. There simply isn't time to co-ordinate all the muscle groups and *consciously* go through all these numerous moves.

So, if we are being indoctrinated to put ourselves through specific contortions by NUMBERS then the general standard will remain in the same appalling state, and fewer people will take up this game "because of it being so complicated".

The answer, I am convinced, lies in HOW we teach the game. Now, before I am inundated with irate letters from teaching professionals everywhere, let me say that there are many fine teaching professionals in Britain who have helped their pupils enormously, who have built a good rapport with them and who have guided them honestly and wisely.

Also, you might rightly ask, "Who are you to tell them what to do and how to do it?" Accordingly, in this and future articles, I will describe *my* method of helping my own pupils and the groups who attended my residential golf schools.

First, let us look at one or two facts and realities. It is a great human trait to put things into pigeon holes and/or categories. Although we live in a liberated, classless society (well virtually) it is good practice to do this, if only to show our colours and to recognize ourselves and the things with which we are dealing.

In golfing terms, and to help you benefit from these articles, this means that it would help if you recognize which of the following categories you fall into.

I think every teaching pro will agree with me that, while beginners come for lessons, golfers with a handicap of 10-15 tend to go "solo". Some do so because they imagine they are not good enough. Most would probably admit to being scared of taking a lesson in case the pro pulls his swing apart and makes them start all over again. This golfer would prefer to study books and magazines in the privacy of his home, in search of that secret move to make his dreams come true.

One other reason why the overall standard of golf is poor is that many golfers play the game simply to enjoy the fresh air and the companionship of others. Providing they hit the occasional good shot they don't really care about getting it round in par. This type of person probably considers that they "started too late" – or they "should have started when they were 8" – or "didn't have the time!"

This type of golfer doesn't want to know about pivoting the hips, ninety-degree shoulder turns, pronating the hands, splayed elbows, etc., and rightly so – but I cannot believe he or she wouldn't like to be better.

And what about you, sir, or you madam, who LOVES the game of golf and reads every written word? It seems slightly unfair that, while the game has become the very corner-stone of your existence you are having to wait so long to break 100.

Or are you the type who can knock it around in 85 in a friendly, but go through all kinds of torment in a medal? If you can recognize yourself, then rest easy. Sit back and enjoy what I have to say. You will improve without consciously re-modelling your swing.

THE SWING

FACT 1. The purpose of the golf swing is to present the clubface square to the target at impact, and travelling in the direction of the target at impact – at speed. HOW YOU DO THIS IS OF NO CONSEQUENCE SO LONG AS YOU DO IT REPEATEDLY.

FACT 2. YOUR NATURAL, FREE-FLOWING, MOST COMFORTABLE SWING is the only one which repeats itself.

FACT 3. Any physical movement induced by CONSCIOUS THOUGHT IS INEFFICIENT. (BBC TV, "The Brain.)

FACT 4. You don't need INSTRUCTION on how to swing the club – you require a little INFORMATION and an EASY MIND.

There is nothing revolutionary about this series of statements. Over the next months I shall discuss them in depth and also comment on:

- How to compete
- The mental side of golf
- How to raise your potential.

I do feel that a much more basic and simple approach is necessary if standards of play, at all levels, are to improve.

Just over a year ago I was fortunate enough to be in Spain and found myself in the magnificent Aloha Golf Club searching for a Barnham Broom bag tag among the many hundreds which adorn the bar (at least that's my story!) when, as always happens there, I bumped into a pal I hadn't seen for some years.

I remembered him not so much because he was a close friend but because he was, as I remembered him, one of the most natural, gifted, golfers I had ever met. Before turning professional he represented England at nearly all levels and his future as a tour player looked good.

Now, here he was, some six years later, having failed to retain his tour card for the second year running, having lost his sponsor, and wondering what to do with his life in the coming year.

When he went to the practice ground to hit some balls I watched in astonishment as he heaved and battered, and twisted and turned. Obviously, I had to ask him what it was he was trying to do! I forget his reply as he slammed another 7-iron twenty feet off the ground in a huge curve which ended up 30 yards left of his target – but I do remember it was a "colourful' reply.

I reminded him that the purpose of the golf swing was to deliver the clubface square to the target at impact, travelling in the direction of the target at impact –at speed.

I further reminded him that how he achieved this was of no consequence at all; that he should first TRUST his NATURAL SWING AND LEARN FROM THE SHAPE OF THE SHOT.

It took several more shots and much reassurance from me before he began to swing the club freely again. Once he began to do this, then we were able to learn from the shape of the shot, and his confidence improved.

By making a small adjustment to his grip and using his NATURAL SWING he managed to get more elevation and less side spin.

A further adjustment to his AIM resulted in some very satisfying accurate shots.

To relieve the anxieties of possibly hitting another hook I asked him simply to be aware of the club head passing through the ball – NOT TRYING TO DO ANYTHING, but to observe.

All the ELASTICITY of his swing returned.

The very easy rhythm and effortless power came back, and it was good to see him smile again.

We went back to the clubhouse (where, incidentally, I found a Barnham Broom bag tag) to discuss the reasons for his previous lack of form. "Quite simply," he said, "I started to listen to everyone. I even bought books because everyone else seemed to know how to play these shots. I didn't. I played them by instinct and feel, but I didn't know why they came off or how I played them."

It was plain to see that the more he learnt HOW, the harder he would TRY. The more he tried, the less he TRUSTED his swing, and the worse he became.

The lesson to be learnt here is to SWING the club FREELY and COMFORTABLY (head still, firm base) and LEARN FROM THE SHAPE OF THE SHOT.

How one holds the club will influence how the clubface meets the ball. The shape of a free-flowing swing will be influenced by:

— Aim
— Stance
— Ball position in relation to stance
— Posture

So will its EFFICIENCY

"Comfort ... Is the Key"

May 1983

"I CAN do it when the ball isn't there!"

How often have I heard that cry? My response is generally the same. "You believe you have the natural capacity to swing the club freely – YOU DON'T BELIEVE THAT IT IS EFFICIENT. So, you TRY to put yourself through a series of contortions and positions when making a shot.

Witness the scene at the first tee of any golf club in the land and you will see the friendly four-ball warming up. Almost without exception the players make a smooth take away and a full turn of the shoulders, followed by a crisp "swish" through the imaginary ball. The club head brushes the grass and the golfer ends up with a high "T.V." finish. Usually there is much joviality and everyone is put at ease.

Witness the scene a moment later and what do we see? "Charlie" steps on to the tee. All is quiet. The smile of a few seconds ago disappears and his countenance changes to one of grim determination. He glares down the fairway, jaw set. Carefully adopting his stance, he places the club behind the ball.

The grip tightens, as do the muscles in his forearms. The tension he feels spreads to the back of his neck and deep into his back between the shoulder blades.

"Come on Charlie," he tells himself, "don't hit it into the right rough like you usually do. Keep the left arm straight, turn the shoulders 90 degrees, hips 45 degrees ... head down, now ..."

His thoughts for the backswing are matched only by his thoughts on the downswing ... "slide the hips laterally to the target, clear them through the ball and kick the right knee in for greater power and accuracy" etc. etc.

As the ball careers into the right rough he is informed that he didn't get his thumbs underneath the shaft at the top of the backswing! As he trudges down the fairway he is filled with an even greater resolve to include that little bit in his next swing.

When he finally finds his ball, however, it is nestling *down* in the grass, and he proceeds to give himself a whole new series of instructions on how to make the shot. "Josephine" on the other hand is happily on the fairway and feeling great. She remembered to dip her shoulder into the ball! Little does she know of the disasters which await her later in the round.

FEAR and ANXIETY cause this Jekyll and Hyde change in us. It is because of our worry about the outcome of the shot that we TRY to GUIDE, STEER and CONTROL the club. The confidence we feel in our practice swing is consumed by doubts and uncertainties when we come to hit the ball.

The problem, of course, is that whilst the practice swing is easy to do without a ball there is no proof that it works! One must wonder, therefore, why you make one when you are going to do something else when making the shot.

This all stems from a lack of understanding of what affects the direction of the shot and the spin on the ball. My pupils laugh when I say it, but also admit it to be true, that most golfers LOVE the game of golf but HATE hitting golf balls!

So, BELIEVE right now that your *natural, comfortable* swing is good enough but that its efficiency is directly related to:

1. YOUR GRIP
2. YOUR AIM
3. YOUR STANCE
4. THE BALL POSITION IN RELATION TO YOUR STANCE
5. YOUR POSTURE

I put my pupils at ease by encouraging them to SWING THE HANDLE ANY WAY THEY LIKE –so long as it is *comfortable*. While keeping equal pressure on the handle with all the fingers of each hand, and keeping the head *still* (not down), they have free license to do whatever comes naturally. They are usually pleased when they see themselves on video!

We are taught to PLAN our shots. Fine! Let's plan WHERE to dispatch our shots, not HOW.

GRIP

The purpose of the golf swing is to deliver the clubface square to the target at impact … How you hold the club will influence how the club face meets the ball IF YOU SWING FREELY.

Most golfers think they hold the club perfectly. THEY DON'T!

Take your left hand (Left handers, the other one for you)) and hold the grip of the club as you would a pistol. Notice how the last three fingers hold the butt, the forefinger loops around the trigger and the thumb settles just to the right of the hammer.

Now take the right hand and assume a "handshake" position. Allow the little finger to fasten itself to the forefinger, and notice how the club is held in the CROOK of the middle two fingers – not the ROOTS. Notice also how the thumb and forefinger settle comfortably into position.

Hold the club in both hands away from the body (club parallel to the ground) and notice how the back of the left hand, the palm of the right, and the bottom edge of the club all face the target.

IT IS LOGICAL TO ASSUME THAT IF WE SWING THE HANDS AND ARMS FREELY whilst keeping equal pressure of the fingers on the handle throughout, THE CLUBFACE WILL RETURN SQUARE TO THE TARGET AT IMPACT

AIM

I feel that, if I were an optician, I would be a millionaire judging from the number of pupils who have difficulty aiming themselves and their swings. This is due largely to having a poor grip, but even more so to a poor ADDRESS PROCEDURE.

Whenever golf is being televised, I encourage my clients to observe how the pros prepare for the shot. Almost without exception they adopt the same procedure, regardless of who it is or how they swing.

They stand behind the ball facing the target so that they, the ball and the target are in one line. (This will help them to "orientate" and plan their shot).

With the hands already in position on the club they take a wide berth, and approach the ball and "target line" from the side.

With weight on the right foot, they lean over and place the clubface behind the ball (keeping both hands on the handle). *They aim their shoulders and clubface together.*

Keeping their shoulders and clubface on line they adopt a *comfortable* stance. If the shoulders are on line they will look OVER the left shoulder to the target – not AROUND it. (Trevino PLANS to play his shots from left to right, hence the reasons he aims his swing with an "open" address position i.e. aiming left of target. Bobby Locke PLANNED to play his shots with a strong draw from right to left, hence his "closed" address position).

STANCE

The width of your stance will influence the shape of your natural swing.

Stand comfortably to the ball with the feet approximately shoulder width apart and FEEL THE GROUND BENEATH YOUR FEET.

BALL POSITION IN RELATION TO STANCE

How the clubface meets the ball, i.e. open, square, or closed to the target at impact, is directly related, not only to how you hold it, but also to where the ball is positioned in relation to your stance.

If the lines across your shoulders, hips and toes are all at RIGHT ANGLES to the leading edge of the club, you will find that:

For a wood, the ball will find itself near to, or opposite, your left heel or in-step.

For a wedge, the ball will find itself in the centre of your stance.

See what happens if you place the wedge off your left foot and the wood off the centre stance. The shoulders and club face of the wedge would aim left. The face of the wood, off-centre stance would aim right.

There cannot be any way of measuring this, since we are all built differently, but if you adopt the set-up procedure as I have described, you will automatically arrange your stance with the ball in its true position.

PLACE THE CLUBFACE BEHIND THE BALL (keeping both hands on the handle).

AIM THE SHOULDERS, then ADOPT A COMFORTABLE STANCE. You will notice a difference in your shots.

POSTURE

The shape of your natural swing is influenced by how you stand to the ball.

We can only be ourselves! How can we stand like Tom Weiskopf when we are built like Trevino? Address procedure (as described) will already have improved your posture at the ball:

a. Your aim will be true
b. Your stance will be firmer
c. The ball position will have found its own station.

More importantly (if this is possible) you will be standing at a comfortably self-regulated distance from the ball regardless of which club you are using.

i. Use your height. Stand tall
ii. Lean over from the hips, allowing the arms to hang freely and knees simply to flex slightly.
iii. Make space between the hips and hands – so move your hips back out of the way. The small of the back will be a little straighter as a result and this will allow your hands and arms to swing freely, more independent of the body.

The definition of POISE is to "hold in a balanced, steady position". How else can you swing freely and comfortably?

All of the foregoing is basic information but it will greatly increase your chances of making more successful shots.

With the correct "address procedure" you may TRUST your swing and LET GO, and thereafter LEARN FROM THE SHAPE OF THE SHOT. Let the swing be COMFORTABLE. That is the key.

Learn from the Shape of Your Shot

July 1983

A. The more forward the ball is in the stance the more "open" the shoulders become at address.

The ball in the final analysis is still your best instructor. So too is your divot.

To learn from the shape of your shot you must first understand what happens at impact to make the ball fly in a given direction, or spin in a given fashion.

This month we shall look at the causes of various types of shots and how they are related to ball position and set up. We will see how, in changing the set up and by USING YOUR COMFORTABLE FREE SWING (*the one which repeats*), the angle of attack and direction of swing will automatically change the shape of the shot. Remember, the cure does not come about through any "secret move" during your swing, but that the shape of the shot is related to how the clubface meets the ball at impact and in which direction it was travelling at the time.

B. To cure a slice move the ball back in the stance

21

THE SLICE

The ball starts off to the left of the target and swerves in a left to right arc, finishing to the right of the target.

The more lofted the club the *less* SIDESPIN is imparted on the ball.

The less lofted the club the *more* SIDESPIN on the ball.

C. A pull results when the swing path is left of target and the clubface at impact is square to the swing path.

Hence the reason golfers will SLICE with their driver and No.3 wood (not so much with their No.4 & 5) and with their 2, 3, 4, & 5 irons. Their favourite clubs will be usually No. 6 & 7 irons because, being more lofted, they naturally impart more BACKSPIN which keeps the ball straighter.

The "slicer" will generally miss the target on the LEFT with their 8, 9 and Pitching wedge because being the most lofted clubs, and by virtue of their being shorter and more upright than the rest of the set, much more backspin is imparted on the ball, causing it to go in a straight line to the direction of the swing.

Assuming that you are swinging the club freely let's now look at the reasons for the slice.

The ball position in relation to the stance may be too far forward. The more forward the ball is in your stance the more "open" the shoulders become at address, i.e. the line across the shoulders will point to the left instead of "parallel with the ball-to-target line".

The line across your toes and hips may well be parallel to the target line but the direction of your shoulders will be aligned to the left, and therefore IN RELATION TO THE TARGET your swing will be steeper, causing a deep divot which will point to the left.

D. The ball fades when the swing path is left of target, with the clubface open to the swing path.

Because of your set up as described, resulting in a "steep angle of attack," your clubface (woods and irons down to 5 or 6) will come to the ball in an "open" position. You can't help it. Any golfer, no matter how good he is, will automatically slice the ball with the longer clubs from this address position.

THE CURE

Move the ball back in the stance (notice how the shoulders automatically square themselves up). TRUST YOUR SWING and LET GO. The ball will naturally set off either in the direction of, or slightly to the right of, your target.

Now watch how the ball curves in the air. The sidespin only takes over once the pace has gone out of the shot. If the ball drifts to the right MOVE BOTH HANDS TO THE RIGHT, slightly. TRUST & LET GO – BE AWARE OF THE CLUB PASSING THROUGH THE BALL. Your "angle of attack" will be shallower and your divot, pointing this time to the target, will be less deep.

Remember that the purpose of the golf swing is TO DELIVER THE CLUBFACE SQUARE TO THE TARGET AT IMPACT – TRAVELLING IN THE DIRECTION OF THE TARGET AT IMPACT – AT SPEED.

To ensure that you are SWINGING the club freely with your hands and arms stand with your feet together and make your shot. If you lose your balance you can't be swinging freely enough i.e. there will still be tension in your shoulders during your backswing and/or downswing.

THE PULL

The ball sets off left of target and holds this line all the way. The swing path is left of target and the clubface at impact is square to the swing path.

THE CURE

Move the ball back in the stance, thus brining your shoulders and, therefore your swing path, on line to the target – TRUST & LET GO.

THE FADE

Once again, the ball sets off left of target and instead of swerving violently, the ball drifts slightly to the right. The swing path is left of target with the clubface, at impact, OPEN to that swing path.

There is nothing wrong with this type of shot: indeed many tour professionals prefer to play their golf with this shape of shot. The example that comes to mind immediately is Trevino.

If you do play this way you must settle for losing distance. However, in certain circumstances it is more prudent to play the ball this way. e.g.

1. In a strong right-to-left wind.
2. When playing to very fast greens
3. At holes where all the trouble is down the left side of the fairway and green.

If, however, you are playing this shot all the time, and wish to DRAW instead of FADE then, as for the SLICE and PULL, you must bring the ball back in the stance and, for the longer clubs, move both hands over to the right a little so that you can deliver the clubface square to the target at impact NATURALLY. TRUST & LET GO.

As I have stressed in previous articles YOU DO NOT NEED INSTRUCTIONS ON HOW TO SWING THE CLUB – you already have the capacity so swing it freely, and so all of the above is INFORMATION on how the clubface at impact, and the swing path at impact, affects the shape of the shot.

Again, I must emphasize, and I tell my pupils and those who come to my Residential Golf Schools time and time again, that YOU WILL NEVER KNOW HOW GOOD YOU COULD BE UNTIL YOU LET GO OF YOUR INHIBITIONS – AND LEARN FROM THE SHAPE OF THE SHOT.

The fact is that most of our mistakes occur in the address position before the swing even begins.

Feel Your Way to a Better Swing

August 1983

- Good golfers generally DRAW the ball
- Good golfers generally have good looking swings.
- Good golfers SWING the club freely with their hands and arms, allowing for a full turn of the shoulders.
- The purpose of the swing is to deliver the clubface square to the target at impact so that it is travelling in the direction of the target at impact – at speed.

purely spontaneous reactions to swinging the club freely.

No matter what your shape, size or stature, you have the capacity to swing freely – the SHAPE of your swing will be influenced by your physical makeup as well as by your grip, aim, stance, etc.

Some of you who have been following this series of articles may still be having difficulty in "experiencing" a free, uninhibited swing, and this *could* be due to the manner in which you trigger off your action.

Learn to Swing the ball freely with your hands and arms allowing a full turn of the shoulders.

Many handicap golfers pick up the club during the takeaway with disastrous consequences.

The above observations are all inter-linked but the "reason why" is contained in the fact that golf is a Bat & Ball game. All the contortions and manoeuvres we make (the head still and body turning "in time") are

I talk about golf being a HANDS & ARMS game. Indeed, it is and the backswing, therefore, should be a HANDS & ARMS movement – albeit that the Body turns to accommodate this action; they go together.

Many pupils come to me in the beginning with either a:

- PICK UP
- FLICK (of the wrists)
- HOIST (upward swing of the arms with no turn of the body)

Seldom with a SWING.

So, by CONCENTRATING & BEING AWARE I want you to make your golf shot, focusing your attention on the FEELING you experience at the start of the takeaway. You will be totally relaxed because all your attention is being focused towards OBSERVING something – NOT TRYING TO DO ANYTHING. If your observations (feelings) tell you that you *are* breaking your wrists immediately on starting the backswing, then play another shot and focus your attention on those muscles which make the hands flick the club head away. Do this several times.

DO NOT TRY TO CORRECT THE FAULT. DO NOT GUIDE OR STEER THE CLUB BACK.

Simply find out which muscles generate the breaking of the wrists. Ask yourself the question:

"What will it feel like to swing the ARMS & HANDS TOGETHER on the takeaway?" LET GO & FIND OUT. Then swing to the finish, observing the club head passing through the ball.

You will discover that by concentrating in this manner your fault will cure itself WITHOUT CONSCIOUS THOUGHT.

Relate your swing to feel.

Remember that "fluffed" shots or "bad 'uns" are brought about through anxiety and tension ... the fear of failing, of ridicule etc. etc.

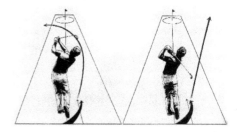

Left: When a player hooks it is generally because the swing path at impact is to the right of the target with the clubface closed to the path.

Right: When the swing path at impact is to the right of the target with the clubface square to that swing path, the result is a push.

Knowing that you are likely to "snatch" (at the beginning of the downswing) your long irons or fairway woods, ask yourself the question:

"At what precise moment during the swing do I feel I want to "snatch" at the ball?". LET GO & FIND OUT.

Your mind, being fully relaxed in looking for that precise moment, is at ease.

There is no room left in your mind for doubts and anxieties about the outcome. No anxieties, no "snatch".

Similarly, with tension in the back and/or shoulders – again an anxiety about losing control and "getting it wrong":

QUESTION. "At what point in my backswing do I feel the tension coming in?" LET GO & FIIND OUT.

Complete awareness of the feeling banishes all fears for the outcome of the shot and the result is a free-flowing swing.

Having enjoyed the feeling of your free-flowing swing, then you can learn from the shape of your shot and make such adjustments to your set up, or grip, as may be necessary.

Last month we looked at the Slice, Pull and Fade and discovered that in all of these cases the swing path or direction of swing at impact was to the left of target, the prime cause being that the ball was positioned too far to the left in the stance, resulting in the shoulders being "open" to the target at address (i.e. aiming left).

We learnt something about side spin and back spin, and how spin is related to the loft of the club and the angle of attack (steep or shallow arc), so it would not come as a surprise that if we over-correct the ball position and grip, we will HOOK or PUSH the ball.

HOOK

The ball starts off to the right of the target and swerves violently to finish on the left.

The swing path at impact is to the right of target with the clubface closed to that swing path.

The ball could be too far back in the stance, causing the shoulders to aim to the right and, if the grip is too strong, the ball will fly in a low trajectory with the long irons and woods, curving to the left – counter clockwise spin having been imparted on the ball as the club face was closed at impact. The Hooker will miss on the left with lofted shots.

WHY? – Because there is more loft on the face, therefore more BACK SPIN is imparted on the ball and it will fly more true to the swing path (or direction of swing at impact).

CURE

Position the ball a little nearer to the left foot (experiment) – pro rata for all clubs – and move *both* hands over to the left on the handle gripping, perhaps, a little firmer with the right hand. TRUST & LET GO.

PUSH

The swing path at impact is to the right of the target **with the clubface SQUARE to that** swing path.

This is really a "good shot badly aimed". Assuming you are now swinging the club freely with the

HANDS & ARMS (loose shoulders), a small adjustment to the ball position at address will bring your shoulders back on line to the target.

TRUST YOUR SWING & LET GO.

As I have pointed out in previous articles the shape of your swing is very much influenced by your grip and set up at address, whether you be short or tall.

The golfer who slices, pulls or fades the ball swings the club on a steeper plane (ball too far forward and shoulders "open"). The golfer who hooks or pushes the ball has the ball too far back in the stance (shoulders closed so aiming to the right).

The plane of your swing therefore is a direct result of the shoulder position at address, and that is influenced by the ball position in your stance.

Your set up determines what happens next!

The flight and spin of the ball will tell you all you need to know and your divot, or lack of it, will confirm your diagnosis.

So, enjoy each swing and look for the "feel" – then learn from the shape of the shot.

Think of Laura

Sept 1983

All of us have feelings. Some people are easily hurt or moved, and are sensitive and emotional, whilst others are less so. Some people are more aware of other people's feelings, whilst others are less so, but even the most hard-hearted of characters will feel pain if they bang their head getting out of the car!

Feelings are EXPERIENCES, either emotional or physical. Sometimes we bite our tongue (and feel the pain) rather than say something which might offend or hurt someone else's feelings – sometimes we say or do things without thinking which do upset – and then we feel sorry, wishing we hadn't been so hasty.

FEELINGS encompass us during all the hours we are awake – they are with us all the time, although for most of the time we are unaware of them as we go about our day's business. For instance, you may be driving your car. You may FEEL excitement at the possibility of concluding a sale, or apprehension at attending an important interview, and all the while your mind hops along from one thought to another as you drive along. If the radio is on or you are talking to your passengers your mind, happily (or otherwise), will wander from one subject to another; yet all the while you are driving your car, slowing down, overtaking, changing gear.

What does it feel like to change gear? You probably don't know because it has become such an automatic reaction and you would probably need to focus all of your attention on the feelings you experience in performing this simple act. If you *were* to concentrate you would begin to notice all sorts of things like the resistance of the clutch pedal against your foot; the muscles of the leg and bending of the knee – feelings that have always been there but have been totally suppressed by other *emotional* feelings.

At a recent Golf School I gave my usual first morning chat on the itinerary for the course and on how each of us would discover how good we REALLY are once we learn to LET GO of our inhibitions, when I noticed a really anxious frown on the face of one of the participants. "You look worried" I said. She replied that she felt nervous of perhaps being too awful to improve and of being the worst golfer in the group.

I had to smile because I have heard this so often in the past and I said, "But don't you feel better now that you have owned up to this worry and have brought it out into the open?" She had to smile too, and immediately felt better about the whole thing. I think the others in the room felt more at ease also. Within the space of a few seconds this lady had experienced two entirely opposing feelings. Her attitude changed from being worried, doubtful and anxious, to being more at ease, interested and curious to learn how she would improve. By owning up to her fears she became ready to learn – to find out.

Later on, when we were on the practice ground, the same lady was struggling to get the ball airborne and was obviously trying hard to do all the things she felt she was supposed to be doing. After all she had had several lessons and collected numerous books and magazines to improve her game. I stood watching her hit a few more balls along the ground noticing how set her face was and how tense she looked throughout. Finally, I said, "Show me how a GOOD golfer would swing". "How can I?" she replied "I'm NOT a good golfer". "Suppose you were Laura Baugh," I countered, "how would you do it?" She looked puzzled, thinking I had flipped too early in the week, but went along with the exercise. She made a full free-flowing swing of the club with all the grace and poise of a winner on tour. I told her that she gave a pretty good impression of a good golfer's swing and why shouldn't we do the same thing with the ball? Immediately she got worried and tense again. "Remember," I said "we're only PRETENDING – it really doesn't matter if you miss it." "Well if we are only pretending and it really doesn't matter what happens, here goes" she said. *She played the golf shot of her life.* She looked stunned, as though a thunderbolt had hit her on the back of her head. I let her take it all in for a few seconds then said, "That is how good you *really* are."

"How did it FEEL?" I asked (*she was still in a state of shock*). "The swing, how did it FEEL?" "I don't know – I didn't feel anything" she replied I asked her to swing again stressing that it didn't matter where the ball went but to concentrate on what she felt *during* the swing. She played another good shot, almost as good as the first. "Easy" she said, "I felt no tension. My swing felt ELASTIC." I asked her to focus on the club head during the next swing and to tell me what she felt. Again, her swing looked at ease, the expression on her face relaxed. She hit another good shot. "I could feel the weight of the club head at the end of the backswing and, again, at impact with the ball", she said, almost totally ignoring the result of the shot.

I suggested that she kept up the pretence of being a good golfer and simply to observe what she felt each time. The result of the shot was to be unimportant for this exercise. I left her to attend to others in the group but when I returned sometime later she was looking dejected, disappointed and very frustrated. Once again her swing had become tense and restricted as she nobbled one along the ground. "Where did the good golfer go?" I asked. "Oh, I stopped playing that game because after a while it no longer worked for me." I explained that her mind possibly got bored with the exercise and that she might well have begun *trying* to repeat the good shots rather than observing the feelings of her swing.

She hit a few more shots (bad ones) and then I asked her to tell me

at what point during the downswing did she feel any interferences coming in. Another bad shot! "During the downswing", she said. "Repeat the exercise," I said "and tell me which muscles are interfering." A better shot followed. "I feel tension in the shoulders early on in the downswing." We're back in business, I thought. She is concentrating again instead of TRYING HARD. "Tell me *precisely* at which point in the downswing you feel the tension in your shoulders." The tension disappeared from her face as her curiosity took over. *She hit another super shot.* "I felt no tension that time – the whole swing felt easy. I also felt the weight of the club head that time, too."

By relating her swing to FEEL she had eliminated the source of her anxieties, i.e. her doubts about her ability to hit another good shot. By relating her swing to FEEL she discovered how good she REALLY was. By relating her swing to FEEL she achieved a state of RELAXED CONCENTRATION and was able to LEARN.

Later on, she complained about hitting good shots off target – but she was having fun – so I encouraged her to adjust her aim and set up and to Let Go and learn again.

A few good shots later I said, "Good 'ere innit?" She grinned.

Feeling Like Playing Well

October 1983

Many of the world's great players talk of the feelings they experience when they are playing well. Some feel that when they arrive at the end of the backswing they are coiled like a spring, others feel that at the same point their right shin, knee and thigh are firm and solid, whilst others again might feel the left shoulder coming around under the chin or even the right shoulder moving away from the ball.

These are "vibes," or impulse feelings as the swing is happening. The tragedy is that when some analyst reports on the subject, highlighting the various positions where those players FEEL whatever it is, the club golfer sets out to imitate the various movements, positions and contortions – and here we are again trying to swing the club by numbers.

I have stressed in earlier articles that so long as your grip is good, your aim is true and your posture correct, you will go through similar contortions as those great players, IF YOU SWING FREELY. It is worth noting that ALL good players swing the club ON ONE AXIS, i.e. the head remains still and the base is firm. You too will experience your own feelings at various points during the swing.

One of the reasons why golfers fail to perform to the limit of their potential is that in their anxiety to succeed they steer the club, manoeuvre themselves and go through all kinds of mental hell to bring off the good shots. In doing this they try hard to repeat the good shot, ("Golly, what did I do right that time?") or try hard to correct what they thought on the bad shot. In each case failure is just around the corner because the doubts in their mind inhibit their actions.

When working with my clients I give very, very few instructions. I give them INFORMATION, but I also ask a lot of questions.

Charlie came for a session recently and proceeded to hit some balls. Well aware of all the things he was supposed to be doing he would work himself into a frenzy of frustration, disappointment and despair at his seeming inability to hit the ball well.

As another ball veered off at an even more acute angle (I daren't say the word, so I'll spell it … S:H:A:N:K), so I asked him "How did that feel?".

"Dreadful" came the reply. "How dreadful?" I enquired. "Oh, it just felt awful." I told him to think about the swing again and, this time, to let go of his emotions (fear of repeating the errors, etc.) that cloud the real feedback of the physical feelings of the swing.

Another shot – another one of THOSE!

"It felt TENSE," he said.

"Really? What felt tense?"

"My shoulders."

"Both shoulders, or just one of them?"

"No, my right shoulder felt tense."

"Did it feel tense in the backswing or downswing?" By now he was looking much more interested as he relived the experience of that "swing".

"It felt really tense during the backswing."

"Fine," I said. "What part of the backswing? Was it in the beginning, middle or end of the backswing?"

"I can't remember," came the reply.

"O.K." I said. "Out of nothing except feeling awful we have discovered that your right shoulder felt very tense at some stage during the backswing. Play another shot. DON'T TRY TO CORRECT WHAT YOU THINK YOU DID WRONG, but focus your attention only to that precise moment during your swing where you feel the tension come into that right shoulder."

I emphasized that I wasn't interested in what happened to the ball or in where it went. I wasn't interested in what he thought he should be doing – I was only interested in the precise moment he felt the tension come into that right shoulder.

The next shot was a little better but his swing had slowed down as though he was deliberately holding back. I reminded him to swing the club any way he liked without questioning if it was right or wrong, but to concentrate on where he began to feel that tension – nothing more. The next shot was a beauty.

The look on his face was a picture. "I haven't hit a shot like that for weeks." He said.

His ego was on a flier again, and I thought to myself that we were approaching another crisis point.

"Where did you feel that tension?" I asked.

"Oh, I didn't feel any that time," he said, as he quickly prepared to play another shot.

As he set up to take the shot, I could see it coming ... another S.H.A.N.K.

The disappointment he felt was total. His ego had taken a dive again.

"How did it FEEL?" I asked (timidly – for he was a big fellow).

"B....Y AWFUL!! It felt tense again."

He told me that during the previous swing he was aware of the hands and arms swinging freely through the ball. Thinking that this was the secret move which would solve all his problems he tried to repeat the swing.

Once more I asked him to find out more about the tension. I asked him to detach himself from the importance of hitting a good shot and simply notice the precise moment during the swing that he felt the tension coming in.

Another good shot followed. The satisfaction he felt at making another good shot was matched by his frustration at not being able to repeat it at will.

"You can repeat it," I volunteered. "DON'T TRY. You know there is a tension in your swing when you hit a poor shot. TRUST YOUR SWING & LET GO – get more interested in where you feel, physically, the tension coming in.

Five minutes later he was making good shots again regularly. His swing was free and he was evidently enjoying himself. Every time thereafter during the course of the session that he hit a poor shot he was aware of the tension: aware of trying hard.

The main lesson to be learnt from this is that in trying to succeed we allow the emotional judgment of the result to cloud and eclipse our actual physical feelings.

There can be no room for emotions in golf. Emotions get in the way of the physical feelings and experience of the swing: the REAL FEEDBACK.

SO TRUST YOUR SWING & LET GO. Get interested in what IS HAPPENING, not in what you think should happen.

How to Compete

November 1983

There are many people who are fiercely competitive – who enjoy the prospect of a head to head tussle and who thrive on the pressures of holing that four-foot putt on the final green to win.

This article isn't so much directed at them but at the host of others who would like to do well in competitions but fail.

Learning how to compete can best be tackled if looked at in two ways.

1. Knowing your limitations and trusting your swing
2. Managing your affairs and having a game plan.

Those who have followed these articles may have experienced the satisfaction which "non-interference" can give. It is a stern mental challenge to keep the mind under control for a round of golf but the joy of "letting go" and playing better golf is rich and rewarding. Discovering how good you ACTUALLY ARE is, in simple terms, good fun.

Carrying this *trust* with you throughout a medal round is well-nigh impossible unless you also recognize your limitations.

These limitations could be of age and physique, of distance (lack of it) or ball control. The subject of this article is, indeed, a huge one and it will be obvious to all that the way in which a circuit professional plans his tournament will differ enormously from the way in which a club golfer gets through his monthly medal round.

Few people really appreciate how many hours the successful (and less successful) tournament professional puts in on the practice ground. The popular misconception is that it must be a fabulous way to earn a living; travelling the world, wearing colourful cashmeres, playing on the world's best courses constantly surrounded by the adoring public – all because they happen to hit a golf ball better than most!!

For every winner there are hosts of disappointed "also-rans" who dash off to the next venue hoping that next week will be their week.

Some will genuinely expect to win and feel good about their chances, some will genuinely expect to finish well up in the money stakes while others will be hoping and praying that they make the weekend this time and therefore pick up some money to reduce the losses for the year so far.

These men and women are true gladiators who, if they are to perform well, must work at their trade to attain and retain these qualities so necessary to reach the top of their profession.

Of course, the same applies to any occupation. Quite simply, if you want to be recognized in your chosen career you must work harder and do the job better than the next person. If there is an easier way to succeed, I would very much appreciate hearing from you!!!

So the tournament professionals will hit golf balls for hours every day, in all conditions. They will practice all manner of shots – to such a degree that when the situation arises on the golf course, they have the confidence and trust to let them come out.

Although there is an enormous difference between the club golfer and the circuit professional, and although the TV cameras distort distances on the box, much can be learnt from the manner in which the great players "manage their affairs".

Most of them will have a thorough knowledge of the course. If it is not possible for them to have a practice round beforehand, their caddie will be instructed to pace it out and acquaint himself with all the information regarding distances, trouble areas, undulations on hidden tee shots – in fact everything the player will need to know so that he or she can swing the club freely and fearlessly during the tournament.

Some players win and build their reputations on playing the percentage game – i.e. taking no risks, allowing others to make mistakes. Others win and earn their reputations by playing fearlessly WITHIN THEIR LIMITATIONS.

Nobody wins by trying to play shots which are beyond, or outside of, their capabilities.

Ballesteros immediately comes to mind as the world's most exciting and fearless golfer. He is gifted with a superb physique. His golfing muscles are strong through hitting millions of golf balls. His endless hours of practice have given him a very clear knowledge of precisely what he is able to achieve so that when you and I watch him in amazement, preparing to play a shot that to us is impossible, you can be certain that he sincerely believes it to be within his capabilities. This belief in himself completely banishes any doubts and uncertainties in his mind which might inhibit his swing.

Each golfer, therefore, must recognize THEIR OWN limitations and capabilities based on their own handicap and experience, AND ALWAYS PLAY WITHIN THEM.

Dedicated players will go straight back to the practice ground after their tournament round if there has been a weakness in their game – to repair this thing and end the day on a "higher" note.

Sam Snead was once asked how he managed to keep his swing so finely balanced all through the years and his reply was as simple and logical as his swing.

"If during a tournament round I hit the ball with a hook, or heavy draw, I would go to the practice ground immediately afterwards and practice until I could fade it."

There are two important lessons to be learnt from this:

1. If you haven't brought it with you, you are not going to find your perfect swing in the middle of a tournament round – so do the best with what you *have* brought.
2. Get back to the practice ground as soon as you can to *repair* whatever damage.

As we know, the shape of the shot is influenced by the position of the club face at impact and its swing path - and these are influenced by the grip, aim, stance and posture.

If it is easy for tournament players to slip into bad habits at address, think how much easier it is for the once or twice a week amateur player.

Unfortunately, there is no substitute for hitting golf balls to build your confidence and trust, and discovering the bounds of your capabilities. No amount of thesis or analysis, opinion or conjecture can give this to you. It is something that only YOU can discover.

Once you find out what you are capable of achieving in terms of distance and "performance," you can begin to formulate your "game plan" for competitions. Having decided what YOUR plan is to be, do not veer from it.

So many times I have heard people say how well they were playing and that suddenly EVERYTHING seemed possible – then, finally, they over-reached themselves taking a disastrous eight by going for a shot which was simply beyond their capabilities. Another card ruined and an opportunity lost to lower the handicap or achieve a good placing.

There are many ways of formulating your game plan, some or all of which you may have heard before. **In all cases you should set targets which you know you can achieve.**

The key to performing to the limits of one's potential is through being MENTALLY RELAXED. We can only achieve this state if we feel satisfied that the task ahead is within our capabilities.

In other words, an 18 handicap golfer who sets off in the medal determined to win, just because he has been playing well recently, will surely put himself under enormous pressure to achieve that goal as soon as he has that first double bogey or 3 putts.

The same golfer might feel more at ease by giving himself a target of achieving 5 gross pars in the round – easily achievable for an 18 h'cap player. If he also thinks of HIS PAR for the round as 90 (on SS 72), then the odd double bogey here or there will still give him a net sub-par round.

He must *genuinely believe* he can get 5 gross pars to feel at ease. If there is a doubt then his target will be set at 3 or 4. This 18 handicap golfer then has the luxury of taking 3, 4, or 5 (depending) double bogeys and still play to his handicap. Any golfer playing to his handicap in a medal generally finishes among the prizes and earns the satisfaction of having played the course in "par".

The point of this "game plan" is to remove the panic in the event of a setback; to stop the conversations in the mind; to prevent the doubts and uncertainties about one's ability and consequently destroying one's natural swing.

Golf is basically a game of mistakes! As long as your mistakes are "safe" ones you have another opportunity to recover, and this is how we should consider how we manage our affairs during a round.

Most amateurs waste shots during a round by under-clubbing and finding bunkers, etc. short of the green. It hardly makes sense to thrash a 7-iron as hard as you can, and just making the front of the green, when an easy 5-iron, even struck poorly, will achieve the same result. If it is struck well it will be pin-high or past the flag. Psychologically it is always better to be past the flag

– at least you gave the ball a chance of going in!

So, regardless of what clubs others are taking, play YOUR OWN game. Regardless of how others are playing each hole STICK TO YOUR OWN GAME PLAN and, finally, regardless of the state of the game, NEVER ATTEMPT ANYTHING WHICH IS BEYOND YOUR CAPABILITIES.

Swing the Club Freely

February 1984

The gold swing is a mixture of swinging the hands as high as you can (brown line—1) and turning the shoulders as flat as you can (orange line—2).

I have received many complimentary letters, phone calls and comments since I began writing this series, all of which have given me a great deal of pleasure and personal satisfaction – for which I am grateful (my own self-esteem and my need to succeed being no less than yours!).

The theme of all these communications has been consistent in that these good people have found improvements in their game through a healthier MENTAL APPROACH.

Learning to cope with oneself, the conversations in the mind, and the difficult situations during a round, is vital if one is ever going to play better golf. The more we TRY to do all the things we feel that we *should do* – the more we FAIL.

One of my "communicants" said to me recently, "I have really enjoyed your articles, Peter – they make a lot of sense and I feel I can equate to them, BUT WHEN ARE YOU GOING TO START TEACHING THE TECHNICAL STUFF?"

My immediate reaction was that he had missed the point altogether!

Although he agreed with all that my articles contained, he obviously felt he needed more technical detail on how to swing the club. I might have referred him to another "very technically minded" professional as I have no more idea as to how to swing a golf club than *how one actually walks* or *drinks one's beer.* Both are highly complicated manoeuvres. I have no idea HOW to walk (do I start with my left foot first, or my right? NO IDEA. BUT I SELDOM FALL OVER!).

Since I am not a Medic I do not know which group of muscles coordinates with other groups to turn, twist, hinge, transfer weight, pivot, etc. ALL IN THE SPACE OF TWO SECONDS! But then neither do I know how to stand up from a "lying down on my back" position. But somehow I have successfully negotiated this complicated manoeuvre every morning for the past 40 years! To illustrate what I mean I want you to ask a pal, or your partner, to lie on his or her back on the floor with the arms by their sides in a totally relaxed fashion.

YOU are going to *instruct* him, or her, TO STAND UP. He, or she, CAN ONLY RESPOND TO SPECIFIC COMMANDS – ONE AT A TIME. You, in effect, are THE BRAIN and your subject lying on the floor is the BODY.

Simply to say "STAND UP" can't work because the body doesn't know how without the commands from the brain as to which muscles to move.

Off you go! Don't be late for work, or miss your tee time!

Now, perhaps, you will see what I mean when someone asks me "How do I swing the club?" I reply "I DON'T KNOW."

"Don't think about it," I say to them "but SWING it – COMFORTABLY."

As I have stated several times in recent months your NATURAL SWING – i.e. the one that requires NO CONSCIOUS THOUGHT – is the only one which repeats. How *efficient* it is, is directly related to:

- How you hold the club
- How you aim
- Where the ball sits in relation to your stance
- Your posture

… all of which influence the shape of your swing and delivery of the clubface through the ball.

There is no doubt, however, that poor golf shots are also the result of OVER-TIGHTNESS (as is a poor grip).

All of us know that over-tightness is caused by a lack of confidence and self-belief in our ability to succeed. In the "physical sense" it manifests itself in our strongest muscles of the hands, back and shoulders. Whenever we experience FRIGHT, FEAR or any form of mental stress those muscles tense up and we, simply, become less mobile. HOW CAN WE PLAY GOOD GOLF SHOTS IF WE ARE TIGHT, STIFF AND STRAINED?

All good players swing the club FREELY with a definite degree of ELASTCITY.

I was discussing this point at one of my Golf Schools when, by coincidence, the Bob Hope Celebrity British Classic was being televised, so we watched the play for about half an hour. Having first drawn their attention to the difference in RHYTHM between the swings of the

Pros and the celebrity amateurs it suddenly became patently obvious to my clients how NERVOUSLY the amateurs "swing" (I use the word "loosely!") the club.

Every Pro that we watched in that short time, WITHOUT EXCEPTION, had an easy *fluid, unhurried and totally "GENUINE SWING"*. The amateurs, on the other hand, even including Tarbuck (who is a low handicap player but experiencing at that time an "off" day), HEAVED & SNATCHED. Not one of them, because of tension, allowed their shoulders to turn or trusted themselves to LET GO.

Most "technicians" would agree that the golf swing is a mixture of swinging the arms as *high* as one can and turning the shoulders as *flat* as one can.

… And before my small legion of friends start ringing up to tell me that I am becoming TECHNICAL, let me simply say that *this is what happens* when one SWINGS the CLUB FLUIDLY, WITHOUT TENSION in the back or shoulders muscles.

Whereas the "technicians" would insist that the correct angles and degrees of the arms and shoulders should be maintained for a CORRECT TAKEAWAY, I would say that IF THERE IS NO TENSION ANYWHERE the arms would swing AT THE SAME PACE AS THE SHOUDERS TURN – AUTOMATICALLY … thus maintaining

such angles and degrees (whatever they are!).

Take any good player and, as you soak in the rhythm and elasticity of their swing (*whether it be a quick swing or a slower one*) you will see what I mean about the shoulder turn.

What is the purpose of the backswing? Obviously, you might say "to get some sort of momentum for the through swing." Quite right! But also, to AIM your swing so that at *impact* the *club is travelling in the direction of the target.*

So although it is important that the shoulders are *permitted to turn,* I certainly do not want you to set about TRYING TO DO IT. Why not relate your swing to FEEL; to discover what it is (*if anything*) that interferes with this natural reaction.

The hands and arms together swing the club freely, and assuming a reasonably firm base and still head, the upper body will *automatically* turn "out of the way" twice.

Save for a few years during the middle 60's when some Golf Swing Mechanic invented the *square-to-square method (which was used for a while by the Americans until sore backs, slipped discs and general depressions set in and then abandoned*), the golf swing has remained virtually unchanged since the days of Braid, Taylor and Vardon *et al*. We no longer play in tweed jackets, and the *gutta percha ball* has been replaced by more durable successors. It is true, too, that modern golf shafts enable us to propel the ball further, BUT THE SWING in those days was pretty much the same as it is today – SWING IT AROUND YOUR RIGHT EAR, THEN SWING IT AROUND YOUR LEFT (*the club, I mean*).

It is interesting to note that in 1886 a Scottish Professional by name of Thomas Kincaid wrote, **"The Body must turn to the left in the downswing as it turns to the right in the backswing"**. That was 100 years ago!

I am not a collector of films of golfers of "yesteryear" but I have seen a few: Boros, Hagen, Sarazen, Snead, Cotton, Percy Alliss, Christy O'Connor, John Jacobs and others. I am not "crawling" when I say that Jacobs was a MUCH better player than ever given credit for!

The only noticeable difference in the swings was the plane. The taller players swung the club on a more upright plane than the shorter players, ALL of them WERE AWARE OF THE CLUB MAKING CONTACT WITH THE BALL. ALL OF THEM SWUNG THE CLUB FREELY.

What Are Your Goals?

Do you remember the professional about whom I wrote earlier and of how he had got himself into such a muddle that he not only failed to make a living on the circuit but had lost the right to compete on the Tour? When I bumped into him, that winter at Aloha, he had lost his game and his confidence – and the future was far from bright.

Good news … he is back on track and back on tour having comfortably qualified at The European Tour School in November!!

I saw him recently again and it was a treat to see him so "at ease" and relaxed. I didn't have to ask him about his game – he couldn't wait to tell me about his game, enjoying his golf; striking the ball solidly and scoring well. With his *new mental attitude* he no longer got upset at his mistakes, or bad luck, and it was this, he told me, that led to his recovery.

He certainly looked to be at peace with himself and, if he can set his own Realistic Goals – and time-phase them - he will feature well again in any company.

I like to hear good news, don't you?

GOAL SETTING must be our first objective if we want to get anywhere. Only by writing down our REALISTIC GOALS will we see them clearly and be able to formulate a plan that we can follow.

We must also recognize that improvement won't come immediately and that the road we have decided to travel will be mostly uphill, so it is imperative to TIME-PHASE them (putting dates to "SHORT TERM, MID TERM and LONG TERM accomplishment).

For every person who has trained and worked hard, and who has won through, there are hundreds, perhaps thousands, who fall by the wayside because the going was too tough, or the setbacks too numerous to enable them to sustain the effort.

For that one person, however, comes the honour, the supreme satisfaction, of having "broken free" from the rest of the pack and achieving what he or she set out to do.

The self- sacrifice, the hard work (and disappointments) are forgotten as the player stands on their own *winners' rostrum* whilst the rest if us are left to applaud and make our excuses as to why we were only "also-rans".

I am addicted to most sports on television, whether it be athletics, golf, snooker or rugby. I have revelled in the glory of the Scots notching up 30 odd points at Cardiff Arms Park (Go on! Let me enjoy it – *you* have beaten *us* often enough!) and have leapt out of my chair when Ovett, Coe or Cram have "kicked" on that final bend. I have sat on the edge of my chair more nervously than Higgins himself as he potted his way to another World Championship and "I was there" when Torvill and Dean brought a new dimension to Ice Dancing, and wept happy tears when they achieved maximum marks. When that Union Jack is hoisted above all others I get a lump in my throat.

What are we saluting when "one of us", or "our" team, has won? On the surface we feel excitement that the race or tournament was won by "one of us". We can reflect upon the thrills of the competition from the early build up and razzmatazz to the final stages of the event, but we would be romanticizing if we thought that was all there was to it. The Coe's, Cram's, Faldo's etc. – champions everywhere will look back on those earlier days when they were "just like us" and wanting to be better. All of them must be physically fit and strong in all the right places. The self-denial, the training, the planned diets, the pain; and the doubts, at times, about "is it all worth it?" The setbacks, the injuries, the disappointments - more doubts – the constant driving of the body to reach new limits are the REAL things which every champion has conquered, and which we lesser-achievers salute.

It would be very naïve for people to imagine that "champions" come, ddenly, from nowhere. Maybe they did in the beginning, but they all had a *Dream* – and that led them to ESTABLISH clear GOALS. Equally they all had to be clear about the *consequences* of choosing them.

Faldo wanted to be No.1 in golf; and Cram wanted to be the best middle-distance runner in the world, but if he was not prepared to train hard he would still be making up the numbers with The Gateshead Harriers.

The great thing about life is that, so long as one has breath, it is never too late to want, or to make, progress and to set your own goals. The older one gets, the less far-reaching one's goals will be, but they will be no less real. If you really do have a burning desire to lower your handicap, or perform better in a medal round, be very clear in your mind as to what it may take (*and the sacrifices you will have to make*) to achieve your ambition.

If your Pro has told you that your poor grip is causing the poor results will you really be prepared to work hard at swinging the club freely with the new grip that he recommended – and really getting acquainted with the new feeling this gives? Or will you just "give it a try" on the practice ground and, if it doesn't work, revert back to the one you had before? If you decided "it wasn't worth the hassle" and did revert back, then it would appear you didn't really *want* to improve that much!!

Imagine how satisfying it would be to go back to the practice ground, employing the grip as recommended, and working yourself through the failures and disappointments until you could swing the club confidently with the new one. By that time the change would feel better. Imagine the pleasure you would feel at watching the ball soar true to your target. Imagine.

If you recognize that your attitude becomes *negative* in a medal round, are you really prepared to work on your *mental attitude* that prevents you from performing as you wish? Are you really prepared to increase your levels of *awareness* over longer periods, or will you allow the first "outside interference" to affect you to the point where you "give up" because you think it doesn't work?

Imagine the satisfaction of breaking through this barrier to the point where you really do begin to perform better in your medal rounds. Imagine.

There is nothing more true than that one must experience sorrow before one can appreciate happiness, shed tears to enjoy laughter and experience failure to enjoy success. Happiness, laughter and success mean nothing on their own because they cannot be measured – think about it.

Happiness can only be measured against unhappier times. Success can only be measured against where you have come from, and where it is that you want to go.

The other day, as I was leaving the practice ground after giving a lesson, I passed "Fred", a member (I'll call him Fred) who appeared to be digging his grave judging by the size of the divots he was taking. "Swing a bit steep?" I enquired. "Cor, no" he replied, "I'm really pleased with the way the shots are going – maybe the divots are a little deep, though." I expressed how pleased for him I was that he was striking the ball well and bid him "Good Day".

Fred must have thought about his divots because I noted later in the day that he had booked himself in for a session with me for the following morning. He seemed to be stuck on 21 handicap and hadn't had a lesson from me for almost five years. I looked forward to working with him again.

As we walked over to the practice ground we chatted, and I asked him (as I ask all of my clients) what he hoped to achieve from the session. "My ball swerves violently to the left with my middle and short irons, and I slice my tee shots and fairway woods. I want to cure these things." (No mention of the divots, I thought to myself). "Let's be more specific," I said to Fred. "You want to hit the ball straight or with a slight draw." "That's what I want." He replied. By asking him to declare what he is starting off with, and for him to explain clearly what he would like to end up with he will easily measure for himself his own progress.

This may, at first, seem rather an obvious statement to make but, quite often, we forget what we arrived with and can be dissatisfied with our progress, however slight, until perfection is achieved!

Frequently I get the "YES ... BUT" syndrome. It goes something like this ... "Good Morning, Madam, what can I do for you?" "I can't get the ball in the air." "Fine," I say "You would be happy to hit the ball in the air?" "Heavens, yes" she replies. A little later, "Madam, are you happy that you are now hitting the ball in the air?" "Yes – BUT I'M NOT HITTING IT STRAIGHT ENOUGH." Later ... "Are you happy that you're hitting the ball straighter now?" "Yes ... BUT I'M NOT HITTING IT FAR ENOUGH." (!!??!!) This demonstrates how we often *move the goalposts,* forgetting our original desires and the reason why we came in the first place. BE CLEAR ABOUT YOUR GOALS.

Back on the practice ground I asked Fred to hit a few balls. "Don't *try* to hit them well" I said "Just let the shots come out the way they want." True to his word the ball flies quite low and swerves a lot to the left to miss the green by quite a bit – another big divot. (You've got it – the palm of his right hand was facing the sky when holding the club rather than at the target). I adjust his grip explaining the effect this will have on the flight and direction of the ball. "I can't hit the ball with this grip." "O.K.," I replied "MISS IT IF YOU LIKE, it doesn't really matter, but let's find out what happens". Predictably the next few shots were not good – the ball flying off to the right. "I don't like this grip. I feel I have no control of the club holding it this way". I reminded him why he had come to me, and that if he really wanted to improve he would need to be prepared to work through the early disappointments before progress could be made.

To take his mind off the change to his grip I asked him to SWING FREELY and NATURALLY letting the ball go anywhere – but to be attentive to the club head passing through the ball, nothing more. To make him more interested in this I asked him to rate it each time on a scale of 1-10; 1 for a "low awareness" and a higher number for "greater awareness". His curiosity now aroused, his awareness increased and his shots greatly improved. "I'll give that one an 8" he said as another shot flew straight and high. Several shots later I asked him about the grip. "Oh, that's O.K now, thanks. Every time I'm aware of the club head I hit good shots," he said to himself, almost as though I wasn't there. Strangely, the deep divots had gone too!

His swing is flowing now and the pained expression on his face has gone.

So set goals for yourself. Write them down so that you can see them clearly. Time phase them remembering that *goals are Dreams – with a date attached.*

Mind Control

May 1984

I am no expert on Mind Control but I firmly believe in it. Indeed, when I launch myself into the subject with my clients at Golf School, I am really only one lesson ahead of them – but they are not to know this!

Psychology - the study of the mind – in recent years has become an important aspect in competing and general performance in sport and business. Sports and Business Psychologists/Motivators are inventing themselves and have an ever-increasing number of clients eager to know more.

It seems to me that, in golfing terms, our typical golf teachers have gone out of their way to avoid the subject altogether, instilling in us all instead, the vital importance of learning the intricate, highly complicated, details of the golf swing. This, of course, leads the client to swing by numbers and to think about every phase of the movement; a movement that takes only two seconds to execute.

As you know my belief is that there does exist a *perfect swing* – a swing that is perfect for *each individual*. Given a perfect grip, aim, stance & posture the swing must be natural, comfortable and fluid from beginning to end. It must be *instinctive* rather than be induced by great conscious thought.

Perhaps those "technicians" are, or were, great players themselves – even champions – and unaware of being in control of their minds during their moments of greatness – perhaps, too, unaware of the traumas of self-doubt and uncertainty which beset lesser mortals than themselves. Perhaps they think it strange to talk in any other terms than "straight left arms", "pivoting hips" (O.K. if you want to damage your back), "angles & degrees".

But people aren't machines, and isn't there more to them than angles and degrees? After all, some people believe that it is not only the tides and seas, winds and rain, affected by the moon, but people's moods, too, and therefore our very existence.

Of course we all have minds which affect how we feel, how we perform, how we view others and how we react to others viewing ourselves.

Some people have extremely sensitive minds and "care" a lot. Others are not so sensitive and care not one jot about what others might think, of how they act and perform, or of the consequences of failing. Or is it simply that these persons do not outwardly display what is really going on inside their minds, and that they really are concerned, but are sufficiently in control of themselves that their performance is unaffected?

So, what controls our physical performance? I guess it is the Brain. Well, I *know* it is and for all that I may give the impression, sometimes, of not using it, it is nevertheless there!

It seems like an insult to compare it to a computer since the computer hasn't yet been built that can match the human brain for efficiency,

endurance and scope – although, maybe that day will come!!

I feel I am getting out of my depth now and that *real* psychologists will be writing in from all corners of the globe, but still I have to ask the question: if a computer requires a three-point plug before it can operate what, activates the Brain?

Is it the Mind? Possibly, and there are millions of things which we do each day *without conscious thought.*

We fall asleep in our beds at night and the brain is still working hard. When we are worried we toss and turn, and when we are at peace we have pleasant dreams. It seems to me therefore that it is the sub-conscious mind which activates the brain, which then activates our muscles, enabling us to do things NATURALLY.

The conscious mind, on the other hand, tells you how you *should* do things and fills your head with all of the consequences of failing.

The young executive making that first speech at The National Sales Conference will surely stammer and stutter and drop those carefully prepared notes if he or she listens to their conscious mind. "Speak up, not so fast – are you sure they want to hear this – you're mumbling," it will say to them. "The M.D. and Board of Directors are examining you on the strength of this performance," it goes on, "fail here and you've blown your chances." These "remarks" made by the conscious mind continue until our Sales Executive is now so consumed with doubt, uncertainty and lack of confidence that the speech will sound totally unconvincing.

So, where does this get us? We have two minds and a brain, or is it one mind with two sides to it, and a brain?

We have a brain which sends impulses to the muscles in our body which are activated by the sub-conscious mind – and we have a surface mind which judges and criticizes the performance – or so it seems to me.

I can still cringe with embarrassment at my poor performances at times when I wanted to impress; and agonize as I relive these awful occasions.

Why should my conscious mind treat me this way? Shouldn't it really be on my side rather than working against me?

Was it, perhaps, during those occasions, out of some sort of understanding that I hadn't practiced hard enough, and it was trying to help me along by constantly telling me what to do?

(Turn, wait for it, - go for it – missed it!).

But if that were the case why did it have to remind me that having dropped shots at each of the first five holes, I was unlikely to get it up and down in two to save my par on the sixth?

Finally, when the nightmare was over and I carded an 82, did it try to console me by saying the greens were awful when, in fact, I left my chip shots so far from the hole that it always took at least two putts to get down?

Why couldn't my mind leave me in peace to play as well as when I play with my pals, knocking it round in par? On those occasions it keeps quiet, doesn't tell me what to do or put me under any pressure at all.

Where was my conscious mind when I was *flushing it* round Woodhall Spa and several shots under par in an event? I'll tell you where it was! It was waiting for me on the 17th tee. Standing there at 5 under par, the hole is a short Par 4 with much trouble on the left.

Suddenly it came out of nowhere, "All you have to do is play safe.

You MUST take care to protect this score." So, I half-hit it into the heather and took 7!! Was I disappointed at taking 7? Yes, I suppose so, but what really got to me was that I listened to my conscious mind. I should have taken my driver on that hole that day, I was playing so well.

You see for the whole round up to that point I was at ease. I was interested in what I was doing. I was playing outside of my mind and felt a beautiful "oneness" with my calm thoughts and movements. I felt that I wasn't *doing* anything – it was happening on its own. I simply knew it was going to be good – and it was (up to the 17th, that is!). The feeling was strange, but beautiful; a feeling of being there but not there – of really being involved but detached from everything else.

Winners in golf often talk about *being in the zone* where everything was running on autopilot. Mountaineers have written and spoken of the same "oneness" of thought and movement. This is the depth of relaxed concentration that erases all the perils and dangers of the situation from their minds. There is an almost religious attachment here, it seems to me, – a brush with perfection as the body and mind in total trust and harmony, achieve limits and heights of performance beyond their imaginings.

A famous American Baseball player known for his excellence often experienced a "Home Run" in slow motion. He felt he had so much time to wind up and unleash the bat to the ball and that the ball (football size!) floated through the air to him as slowly as a feather for him to discharge into the crowds at his leisure.

How close to perfection was Beaman, the American long jumper in the Mexico Olympics when leaping 24 feet with his first jump, or, Roger Bannister breaking the 4-minute mile on a cinder track? Would all these achievements have been possible under the critical, judgmental eye of conscious thought?

Perfection, so it seems to me, is everywhere around us. We touch it in moments of the subconscious controlling our actions – we lose it when the conscious mind barges in on the act.

Perfection is a bonny woman walking down the street with all the poise and grace of a beauty queen unaware of the admiring glances.

Perfection is granny knitting the most complicated pattern whilst watching her favourite TV programme.

Perfection is the innocence of a child and the wisdom of the aged.

My conversation with myself has covered a lot of ground – so where have I got to?

We have a brain and a mind that has two sides to it. We have a conscious and a subconscious mind. When there is a oneness (a Trinity) we achieve perfection – or so it seems to me. When the conscious mind dominates us our mood and manner change. We fall pitifully short of the target we set ourselves – and we cease to perform.

It appears obvious now that the conscious mind is not our friend and that we ought to recognize this "foe".

Our conscious mind craves adoration, demands applause, seeks respect of others, wishes to be "tops", hates failure and cannot cope with being beaten. If it thinks that others are better, then it would rather not compete at all in case it didn't measure up. It worries about these consequences and will move heaven and earth to make things better. It cares, not for its own sake, for what others will think of it. Its self-esteem, its ego, drives it to strive so hard. The more it instructs the less it achieves. It is obstinate and persistent. It never lets go. The thing is it knows absolutely nothing about HOW TO DO ANYTHING – but it really wants to help you perform better. It thinks that it can but doesn't know how, except to give you constant instructions.

I liken it to an employee in your own company who is basically, a good person, has a nice family, etc. but the job he or she is performing for you is "rubbish". Rather than sack this person and being the good and wise employer that you are (!?) you find another department for this employee to work in to which he or she is better suited.

Since the conscious mind is a truly awful instructor it is, nonetheless, an excellent "observer" and if we can utilize this "strength" that it has you, and "your company", will perform better. We have to occupy it with something else to do to arouse its curiosity or interest in something while we get on with what it is that we are doing.

Basically, we want to take away the *judgment* of the conscious mind – because this is what it does – perpetually. And, wanting to help you as it does, it bombards you persistently with meaningless technical instructions. You follow its instructions as best you can – "Full turn, weight on right foot, straight left arm, slide and turn etc." and when the ball scuttles away into a bush it will then make judgment on your disappointing effort. "Your swing was too flat and you forgot to use your legs – dummy."

These comments continue for the whole round. Even when you hit that "scorcher" – right out of the screws it will leap right back at you. "Do you want to know what you did right that time? You turned your shoulders better!" So, of course, on the next shot you overdo the shoulder turn with disastrous results!!

So, it seems to me, that if we are to keep the conscious mind under control we mustn't allow it to THINK of anything because to think is to hold an opinion of something, and that is the very thing it is best at.

No, here are a couple of ways of occupying its attention when you play a shot.

1. Swing the club freely simply, allowing things to happen. Do not question what you are doing or how you are doing it. Focus all of your attention on the head of the golf club. Let it go all the way to the end of the backswing and let it swing through the ball to the end of the follow through. Be AWARE of the PRECISE MOMENT the head arrives at the end of the backswing and the PRECISE MOMENT it makes contact with the ball. Remember you are not trying to hit the ball perfectly; you are simply noticing the club in its arc. Mark your level of awareness out of 10. In this way you are detaching yourself from what you *should* do and are observing *what is*.

2. If your swing feels tense find out during the next shot what part of you feels the tension. At what moment during the swing do you feel the tension to kick in? Every time you swing the club mark it out of 10 for the tension. In this way your conscious mind, the arch-critic and "controller" (it thinks/wants to be) is put into "awareness mode".

If your conscious mind gets really interested in these or other exercises, you will truly get "off the surface" as it becomes more deeply absorbed and you will get closer to that detached "oneness" of mind (sub-conscious) and movement – and enjoy the difference in your performance.

Be aware of your thinking. If your expectancy is high you will TRY. Why try when you perform better when you don't?

Let the Real You Shine Through

June 1984

I received a letter the other day from a very special lady, who, having lost many of the early battles, is beginning to win the war.

As I read the words about "this and that" the message between the lines came through loud and clear of a new-found confidence both in her golf and in herself, and I thought back a year or two ago to her first Golf School, when she was battling to find herself - and a golf swing that worked.

We tend to act and behave according to how we feel inside and very often what comes out is not a true reflection of how we really are.

When we feel uncertain about something, we feel tentative. When we want attention because we feel we are being ignored, we behave irrationally. Some people will pour beer over their heads (yes, really) and others will laugh hysterically at the smallest thing, while still others will do something - anything – just to be noticed.

Unfortunately, what comes over to other people who are subjected to this behaviour can be both irritating and tiresome, resulting in their forming a completely different impression of that person to what is *really* there, and the *cry for help* is lost – unnoticed in the behaviour.

What makes us aggressive? Is it a fear of not putting over our case clearly enough in a discussion? What makes us try to impress? Is it because we fear we won't impress by just being who and what we are?

Is it so important to us to make such an impact? Why don't we just let other people form their own opinions if they must? After all they are only *their opinions* and don't affect us at all. So why not just let them form their own impressions of who we *really* are?

All of us react well when we are comfortable, or at ease with what we are doing, or in whose company we find ourselves. Natural laughter, natural conversation, natural behaviour abounds because we feel no need to "perform well". Words and actions come easily the more *comfortable* we feel and it is at times like these that our *real self* comes through to the surface.

One could go on endlessly, and this principle could be applied to all things in life, but since golf for many of us is an important part of our life, our behaviour pattern can vary as to how we feel inside and especially when on the golf course.

Quite often in the past I had to play golf with a businessman important to Barnham Broom in some way, or to my career and, then, it was a problem for me – one with which I had difficulty coping. I felt that I had to impress them with my play, and so from the very first moment I would be keyed up knowing that I hadn't made time to practice or prepare. I hoped and prayed that I wouldn't make a fool of myself. I felt that my own self-esteem and what others thought of me was very much on the line at those times – or so I thought. Was it to be just another case of playing well in friendlies, but of falling apart in a medal?

Looking back now I can smile at the panic I felt in my mind and the agonies I endured, because now I have learnt how to deal with these situations and *be at ease;* and, surprise, surprise, it's funny how I play better, too!

Quite recently I had occasion to play golf with a gentleman who, some ten years ago, was a county player but, because of business and a sore back, now played only occasionally. Some friends had half bored him to death about this "Teaching Pro" and so the only way, he felt, to escape a further "ear banging" was to have a round with

him and get the d.....d thing over with.

We were in the Spanish sunshine (*again! I like it there!*) and watching him go through the motions it was obvious he had played the game well at some stage. Although we were playing for only a Gin & Tonic (or two) his *gentle draw* of the first couple of holes (all square) quickly developed in to a *heavy one*. By the 6th (one down) it became a definite hook. Coming up the 9th (3 lost balls – four down and 5 shots gone) his back was obviously giving him pain, his swing more restricted and his hook unreal – so we retired to the clubhouse promising to meet up again the following morning on the practice ground.

By the next morning his back was feeling better so we loosened up with a few chip shots.

"Why do you think the ball hooked so violently yesterday?" I asked him. "I think that as I was driving my legs my hands were dropping from the 'inside'" he replied. "Sorry" I said "the ball hooked because *your club face was closed to your swing path that was travelling to the right of the target*. No other reason. What controls the club face and what determines the swing path?" I went on

"The left side clearing through the ball" he said. "Wrong again, Sir – your HANDS control the club face and your BODY ALIGNMENT the swing path. Remember that if *the ball swerves to the left move both hands to the left on the handle.* What is the purpose of the golf swing?" I asked him. "To hit the ball" he quite rightly replied. "What with?" I enquired. "My legs" he said. "Your LEGS? Even the greatest golfers in the world hit the ball with a CLUB – which they hold in their HANDS" I said.

I explained that the only purpose of the golf swing is to deliver the face of the club square to the target through impact – at speed. This can only be achieved by the use of THE HANDS. Then it all fell into place. My friend was a student of the Square-to-Square Method discarded by all the great players about ten years ago. "Nicklaus, Weiskopf, Palmer *et al* used this method for a while until, that is, problems with their backs set in." He replied, grinning "Well, at least I was in good company!" "Sure, but didn't they do well to get out, because they are still playing today!"

It may help to imagine that your right palm is the clubhead when you are trying to establish

the relationship between your hands and the clubface.

"If all you are telling me to do is swing the club with my hands and arms" he asked "what shall I do with my legs?" (*The trouble with square-to-square fellas is they have an almost incurable obsession with LEGS!*). "Stand on them," I said "as you swing the club and find out what happens to them. Furthermore," I encouraged "swing the club anywhere both hands and arms want to go *together,* but FIND THE BALL WITH YOUR HANDS." To help take his mind off the surface by trying hard I asked him to be aware of the club head passing through the ball. The shot that followed was sheer perfection! The ball soared over the marker with a slight draw spin.

"Were you aware of the club passing through the ball?" I asked. "I'm not sure. I think so." "Play another," I said "then tell me if you are more aware this time." Another super shot came out – just as before. "I still can't tell," he said with a hint of disappointment. "O.K. but does it matter?" I asked. "The important thing is you got away from *trying* to swing the club well and allowed your natural swing to come out."

I guess he had hit 50-60 balls using all of the clubs without hooking any of them. "How's the back?" I asked. "Feels great., My whole swing feels freer but, now, I tend to hit the ball sometimes to the right." *(Nose fixed – but Mouth doesn't work?)*. "O.K." I said "Establish the relationship between your hands and the club face. Remember, the club face will do whatever your hands do. Be sure that your grip is good. It may help if you imagine that your right palm IS the club face." I explained the only reason the ball went to the right was because the face was looking to the right at impact. Now that his grip was perfect I then I asked him to *really* HOOK the ball out of the park – but from a normal, well-aimed, starting position. Another, and another ... and another great shot soared over the marker in the distance

"How's your back?" I asked. "What back?" he replied, smiling.

Later in the clubhouse we talked about the transformation and I assured him that what we saw out there was *the real person being his true self*. What I saw the day before was someone trying to be someone else; somebody who so lacked the faith in his own natural swing that he adopted another role – unsuccessfully and painfully. Not only was it painful physically, it was painful to his self-image also.

"Be yourself," I said. "Your natural swing will repeat if you get out of your own way mentally and physically. We get in our own way for all manner of reasons – mainly though anxiety – so that we end up becoming other people.

Our uncertainties and lack of confidence in ourselves make us react irrationally, which affects our performance and gives others a completely distorted impression of who we really are.

So, remember my lady at the beginning of this article? Here is the advice that I gave her back then - "Be like this special lady," I said "and allow the good shots to come out by not interfering. Be yourself and let others form their impressions of the *real* you.

Back to the Basics

July 1984

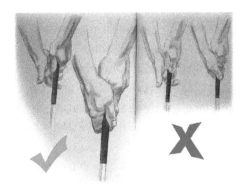

A question I am often asked is "Where should the ball be in relation to my stance?" My reply is usually the same each time, "Wherever your hands tell you to put your feet."

The quizzical looks I get from my pupils when answering in this fashion affords me the opportunity to explain the basic reasons for the set up procedure.

Over the past months I have talked about two things above all others:

To deliver the face of the golf club squarely to the *target* at impact – at speed, and, to *"get out of your own way"* mentally and physically on every shot.

It is very logical to assume, therefore, that the HANDS and ARMS play a vital role in golf.

Too often we allow other things to enter our mind. Things like the *swing plane, keeping a firm right side* in the backswing, *left arm straight.* These, and many other thoughts, creep into our consciousness obscuring the original intention of *delivering the club face to the ball and target.*

Above - To establish a good relationship between the hands and the clubface, I do believe that a proper grip is essential. Notice how the club is held in the middle two fingers of the right hand and not in the roots.

To establish a good relationship between the hands and the clubface I reiterate that a "perfect grip" is essential. Many golfers assume that their grip is good. Many are wrong! When hitting their poor shots they imagine the reason is due to some imperfection in their technique, rather than that their hands are holding the club incorrectly. JOHN JACOBS said many times *"You will never see a "good golfer" with a poor grip – neither a "poor golfer" with a good one."* There is nothing more true.

I stress that the right hand should hold the club as illustrated in the two graphics shown on the left: the club in the crook of the two middle fingers – and NOT the roots. Holding the club in the roots, as illustated in the two graphics on the right, causes the palm of your right hand to look at the sky rather than at the target at address, causing all manner of strange results.

The HANDS most definitely do CONTROL THE CLUBFACE – and the clubface will do exactly what the hands do - if the GRIP IS PROPERLY APPLIED.

So now that the grip IS properly applied it may feel strange to you at first holding it in the crook of the fingers of the right hand. You may feel you have less control of the club and worry, even, at not being able to hit the ball holding it this way.

The underlying problem is that most right-handed golfers are right-handed people and they imagine they need to use the strength of this hand to apply *the force* at impact. This is wrong!

It is the turning of the body twice (*away from the target in the backswing and through to the target in the downswing*) that "fuels and energizes" the SWING OF THE ARMS & HANDS through impact.

So, back to the Set Up Routine. Once you have selected your club and taken your grip (*the "perfect one", mind!*) place the clubface behind the ball aiming at the target. Do this with BOTH HANDS ON THE HANDLE. Without moving the club simply "fashion yourself" around the club and ball until a relaxed and comfortable address position is achieved.

By letting your hands dictate where your feet should go (*so long as you do not adjust the clu*b) the ball will find itself in the middle of the stance for the lofted clubs, and towards the left for the longer, less lofted ones. The hands and arms hanging down loosely below the chin and with the body leaning over from the hips – not the waist – will determine the correct distance to stand from the ball so that everything falls into place naturally at address.

Strange – but every time I have my clients address the ball in this manner, they play better golf shots!

Quite frequently at this point in a lesson, after logically explaining the set up procedure, I say simply, "Get on with it – give the ball a STING."

Some pupils in "getting on with it" will cautiously and deliberately "grind through" all the contortions many instruction-freaks and swing-analysts have recommended for years in an effort to hit the ball, and it is at this point that I mention the calculator. "THE CALCULATOR" you say? "Yes - the calculator." We live in an age of the calculator.

A calculator, as we all know, takes all the information – the input – and at the press of a button produces an answer that we believe to be true. Whether it be the bank balance, or the discount, or whatever else, we only have to press the "EQUALS" button to get the answer – and we never question the answer it gives us.

Amazing things are calculators! Having selected your club and put in your information at address re distance and direction – simply press the "equals" button i.e. TRUST & LET GO and find the ball with your hands.

It is when your own attempt to do the calculation during the swing that things go wrong (*physical movement induced by conscious thought is inefficient*).

I have found over the years I have been teaching that 90% of all golfers are concerned and worried about their backswing. When I look around me everyone, it seems, is practicing the backswing – stopping at the top, looking at their reflection, trying to get it right.

How can one retain a real interest in presenting the clubface to the ball if thoughts of the backswing are nagging at you?

A lady who had attended my golf schools over the past three years and who came to me as a complete novice, spent a week at Barnham Broom recently in her Timeshare apartment and took the opportunity to have me check her swing.

Her game had improved immensely, and she often struck the ball with authority, dispatching it much further than the average lady golfer, but even she went through stages of not trusting her swing. She would fidget and "faff" at address complaining of not feeling comfortable.

On those occasions she would guide, steer and try to place the club in position during her swing and, of course, the results of her endeavours were less than satisfactory.

She would sway, over-swing, hit the ground before the ball on those occasions, complain some more and generally work herself into a frenzy!

I had an old car tyre on the practice ground. Three-time Open Champion Henry Cotton used one for his practice.

"STING THE TYRE WITH THE CLUHEAD" I said. She "poked" at it two or three times until I gently encouraged her to "STING IT, WOMAN." (I don't really shout at my pupils but, sometimes with this one I have to speak louder than her to be heard!).

She became so absorbed in the idea of stinging the tyre that her uncertainties about the backswing disappeared. Her swing transformed into something of technical excellence.

She stung the tyre several times and each time in drawing the club away it arrived at the end of the backswing horizontal; the shoulders had turned fully, her head remained still. Her arms had swung up, her arc was wide. The hips had pivoted and all the other contortions as recommended happened quite naturally.

The more interested she became in "stinging the tyre" the better her swing came out.

We left the tyre and I invited her to sting the ball in exactly the same way. I reminded her that to "sting it" she should use her *hands*.

She made very good contact after that and found her trust again.

As I left her, she was still muttering "THE HANDS CONTROL THE CLUB-FACE – FIND THE BALL WITH THE HANDS".

If that was all that she was muttering then I am pleased!

Check Your Posture

August 1984

Most of our mistakes occur in the address position long before the swing even starts and it is an unfortunate fact that all but the very good players fail to recognize this.

Well, I must believe this to be true since ninety-nine out of every hundred clients who come to me look for "the secret move" to make their swing better and more efficient, when all the time THEIR OWN NATURAL SWING would be much more efficient if the input at address was GOOD.

In earlier articles we have looked at THE GRIP (*which influences where the clubface will look at impact*), and we have talked about BALL POSITION in relation to the stance (*which influences the direction in which the clubface travels at impact*). We have looked at THE AIM.

Since a Free Swing of the arms and hands is fundamental the direction of the swing at impact will be influenced by the aim of the shoulders at address.

Now we must look at how one's POSTURE at address will influence the plane of the natural swing and, therefore, the shape of the shot.

I am getting really well used to the "quizzical", "unbelieving" looks my clients throw at me when I give them free licence to swing the club any way they like. I tell them that so long as the arms and hands swing independently of the body around a still head (*NOT "down"*) and a firm base (*without tension*) they can let the body do anything it wants IN SYMPATHY with that swing. The ONLY thing that I do insist upon is that free swing of the arms. Until we commit ourselves to THAT we can never really learn from the shape of the shot. We shall feel disappointed with our failures – guide, steer and contrive all manner of moves to make the ball fly better until we reach the point where our frustrations take all the fun out of the game.

There are only two key factors, in my view, in golf:

1. *The Shape of the Shot.*

The direction in which the ball sets off tells you about your swing path at impact. And the spin of the ball producing a swerve to the left or the right tells you how the clubface met the ball – whether it was "closed" or "open" to that swing path. If the ball flies straight one must assume that the clubface was square to that swing path at impact.

Forgive me for making the over-obvious statement that the shape of the shot is simply the direct result of the clubface meeting the ball. If that is a really obvious statement then it must be equally obvious that one can alter the shape of the shot, at will, by adjusting one's aim and set up or grip at address!!

"Ah!" I hear you say, "I know all that but I can still slice the ball from any position!" How often have I heard that cry! It is then that the OTHER known factor comes into play

2. *The Physical Experience of the swing.*

Many of us "get in our own way" mentally or physically during the swing. Our thoughts can range from "I must turn my shoulders in the backswing" to "I must get it RIGHT this time". There is nothing surer than that when we continually give ourselves "instructions" *during* the swing, we cease to swing the club freely and independently of the body.

For as long as we TRY to do this or that thing, we get in our own way. For as long as we have doubts and uncertainties about what we are doing, or about the outcome, we become inhibited and get in our own way yet again.

We will never know how good we *might* be until we relax mentally and physically but, of course, until we stop blaming our swing for the poor shots and, instead, adjust the "information at address" we will always be inhibited and will continually try hard – and continue to fail.

The one thing that I nag my clients about, whether they be the juniors I coach at a weekend, the adults who come for personal tuition, or the groups who attend my Golf Schools, is to take a correct grip and adopt a correct Set Up Routine as described often in this series. The benefits of this are quite simple – they increase your chances of playing good shots.

Far too often I see golfers who have a good idea of what a correct grip is, and who recognize the importance of a correct aim and alignment, attempt to put themselves into position BEFORE placing the club behind the ball. All too often they stand either too close to the ball or too far away. Often, they stand too tall or in a crouched position.

Some golfers, in adopting a poor address procedure will do all, or some, of those things during a round. Others will *groove* into a poor "pose" at the ball – out of habit. ALL of them will blame their swing for their poor shots and inconsistent golf.

If you truly are swinging the arms freely and are getting *out of your own way* DON'T BLAME YOUR SWING – have a look at your POSTURE at address.

This influences "the angle of attack" and, therefore, the shape of the shot.

It influences whether your swing is "fluid" and "elastic" or "tight" and "restricted".

When you look at the pros on TV you will notice, almost without exception, that their posture over the ball is one of *straight lines and angles*.

There is a definite impression of BALANCE – SPACE – WIDTH for the arc, and POISE. Some dictionaries define POISE as "to be in a balanced, ready position".

When these good players swing the arms away, the shoulders turn automatically (*in time*), the lower body remains "heavy", the right knee holds its position and the hips *are pivoted*. The whole chain of events,

in the through swing also, is permitted to happen naturally from a good posture at address.

PLEASE DO NOT TRY TO PUT YOURSELF THROUGH THESE VARIOUS MANOEUVRES – THEY ARE AUTOMATIC AND SYMPATHETIC TO A FREE SWING OF THE ARMS.

People who come to me with a poor address procedure adopt one of these postures:

See illustrations 2, 3 and 4.

Illustration 2

This shows the golfer reaching for the ball. Notice how his posture puts his weight on his toes; a feeling of "imbalance". This golfer has difficulty in swinging the arms freely and will, therefore, have too much body-action, causing anything from topped shots, pushed-fades, the occasional "duck-hook" and that other unmentionable shot – and I don't mean a slice, although he will do that as well!

Illustration 3

This player has almost got it right. He is standing tall using his greatest asset of all – his height. Whether you are 4'11 or 6'7 your height is your greatest asset because it influences the WIDTH of your swing and, as we all know (now!) the wider the swing the greater will be the club head speed through impact (IF you swing the arms and hands!).

This golfer, however, is still "getting in his own way" physically and his posture has a letter C look about it. He may even feel too close to the ball and be tempted to move back a little. This would be a shame because he would end up a little like the golfer in illustration 2.

This shows the golfer who was taught to "sit on the bar stool". The plane of his swing will be very upright as he picks the club up. The shoulders will not turn out of the way, thus causing an over-swing on an "out-to-in" swing path. He may slice or top the ball and will certainly never hit the thing very far. He should find a TALLER BAR STOOL and perch on the very edge of it.

All he needs to do is to move his hips back out of the way (or stick the bottom out) thus creating more room for his arms and hands to swing more freely. In moving the hips out of the way his posture will take on that "professional look" and he will sense that "balanced", "ready for action" feel.

When he swings the arms freely without conscious thought, he will automatically go through ALL the manoeuvres and contortions as recommended by those Swing Mechanics. His body will be accommodated by that swing.

Much more importantly – he will increase his chances of hitting better golf shots, of trusting his swing and of playing "outside of his mind".

Illustration 4

66

It goes without saying that although all these illustrations are of men, this applies equally to women golfers, too.

GET OUT OF YOUR OWN WAY – AND GIVE YOUR NATURAL SWING A CHANCE.

Improve without Changing Your Swing

September 1984

Your focus should be on the clubhead arriving at two specific points in the swing – 1. The end of the back swing. 2. The point of contact.

"What should I think about when playing the shot?" It is a question I am asked almost every day and one that lends itself to hours of discussion in the bars and locker rooms, boardrooms and bus queues everywhere. What *should* one think about during the swing?

The subject is such a large one that I am almost hesitant to make these comments. But I do believe that until definite distinctions between CONCENTRATION and AWARENESS are made, then for most of us, golf will remain a very difficult game indeed.

The high handicap golfer searching for the "secret move" will ask the good player, "What do you think about when playing the shot?" and will get not one grain of real information when he or she replies, "Nothing."

Little comfort, indeed, to the poor soul who is searching for that medal score that will reduce their handicap.

Further questioning of the good player will reveal that if they do have a *thought* it is likely to be WHERE they plan to send the ball. On the tee they will have visualized the shape of the shot they want to hit, to suit the design of the hole and the contours of the land, so that they may play their next shot from the optimum position to the green.

Sometimes, of course, he or she dispatches the ball in some other direction, for even the best professionals in the world are fallible, but when this does happen, they simply plan the next shot.

We have seen the pros on T.V. standing beside their ball looking at the situation (*scratching their heads and in deep discussion with their caddie*) and what is going through their minds are all the options open to them at the time. "My lie is good so I can make good contact," or "The flag is just behind the bunker so I will give this one lots of 'air'," might be how their mind will work. Or, if in deep rough, they might weigh up in their mind how far down the fairway they can realistically send the ball in getting it back into play. He or she will seldom be greedy in going for too much distance – experience will have taught the player that the most important thing, when in trouble, is simply to get out of it quickly and assuredly.

Of course, "miracles" do happen, or at least they seem like miracles to us.

Half the golfing world saw an unbelievable bunker shot that Ballesteros played with a No.3 wood which carried 280 yards to the green to keep our Ryder Cup chances alive.

He would never have attempted it unless he felt it was within his capabilities at the time, and I am absolutely certain he would be the first person to advise us lesser mortals, when finding ourselves *off the beaten track,* to get the ball back into play and as far down the fairway as is REALISTICALLY POSSIBLE.

I have long based my teachings on giving your swing a chance by *setting up correctly.* We are, after all,

SETTING UP OUR SWING. Having "set it up" TRUST & LET GO.

Doesn't Ballesteros epitomize everything that message contains?

The good golfers see the situation and PLAN WHERE to send the next shot. They may also plan the shape of it – to hit it with "draw" or "fade" as may be required or to hit it "high" or "low", either depending on wind conditions or in order to go "over or under" trees etc.

THEY NEVER THINK HOW.

The vast majority of my pupils come to me for the very good reason that the ball does not go, often enough, where they want it to.

More often than not their minds are filled with TRYING NOT TO SLICE or TOP the ball, or take divots or whatever else, and when I might tell them, for the purpose of the exercise, they must let the shot come out the way it wants to, the FEAR of doing the same thing inhibits their movements – resulting in a repetition of the same poor shot.

I met a lovely lady at one of my Golf Schools who had broken her wrist some months earlier.

Her backswing was technically good in that her base was firm (*enough*) with the knees slightly flexed. A good shoulder turn produced all the "right moves" of pivoting and weight transfer naturally – but everything seized up in the down swing. She hit "at" the ball as everything tightened up at impact. Naturally she topped a lot along the ground.

It was obvious she was terrified of taking a divot and possibly hurting her wrist. I asked her to swing again. I told her that it didn't matter where the ball went but I wanted her to find out what her FEET were doing during the swing!

She wasn't to try to do anything she thought she ought to – simply to focus her attention to what the feet DID during the swing.

The transformation was astonishing. Her swing became *elastic* and *fluid* as she swung the arms freely through the ball. Her head remained steady throughout allowing her body to clear out of the way as she swung through the ball to the finish. Everything that the "analysts" would say *should* happen happened AUTOMATICALLY. The ball flew through the air and she felt no pain in her wrist.

By giving her a FOCUS (*what her feet were doing*) – something for her to absorb herself in – she allowed her NATURAL SWING to come out without any inhibitions.

She said that she felt her weight transfer naturally from one foot to the other during the swing.

I sensed that she might TRY TO REPEAT the move thinking that this was the *correct thing to do*. If that were the case, she would cease to swing the club NATURALLY and begin to think about *what she should be doing*, so I simply asked her to play some more shots and to find out how much of her weight transferred by the time the club made contact with the ball.

Her expression during the following swings changed from the nervous, anxious frown that she had at the beginning, to one of RELAXED CONCENTRATION as she absorbed herself in the exercise.

"Give it a percentage," I said, "but you will never be able to measure it until you Let Go."

I left her swinging beautifully.

The effect this had on the others in the School when we watched the video film was tremendous. To witness this exercise on film and to see how this lady's swing transformed WITHOUT HER TRYING confirmed two things:

1. You CAN improve without *consciously* changing your swing.
2. Awareness creates concentration which accelerates learning.

Through concentrating in a totally NON-JUDGMENTAL ATMOSPHERE in something other than what she *should* be doing, this lady discovered the technical excellence of her own natural swing. The fact is that TRYING HARD FAILS.

This point is proved time after time again. Some golfers – usually the higher handicap players – try hard most of the time whereas the lower and middle handicap players will find themselves trying only in moments of crisis.

Ian (14 h'cap) was one of the latter category players. He had discovered the joys of *virtual abandon* and was hitting his drives and fairway woods with a draw for the very first time (*much improved grip, aim, stance & posture*). Life was wonderful until he found himself in a greenside bunker. His expression changed to one of serious, grim determination and his first two or three attempts to get the ball out all failed.

"Who is the best bunker player at your club?" I enquired. "Charlie Brown." He replied. "BE Charlie Brown," I said, "the best bunker player in the club."

He assumed the "role" and, thereafter, got out of bunkers every time. No, they weren't always as good as Charlie's – but he got the ball out first time, every time. In taking on the "role" he, simply, took himself *off the hook.*

I can hear some of you scoffing at this nonsense but I do assure you that you can only perform to the levels of how you feel inside.

If you are nervous, anxious or doubtful in any way about the outcome, you will play the shot that way.

Walk away from the fear of failing and look at the other side of the coin – it might be the best shot of your life … so look forward to playing it! FEEL GOOD about it.

This is all well and good for the practice ground you may say, "But what should I think about when playing a round of golf?"

A gentleman started coming to me for help a couple of years ago and at that time he was in a terrible mess. His head had been filled with so much technical information he could hardly take the club back from the ball. He had been taught to do so many things during the swing that he constantly got in a muddle – there being so many things to think about (*paralysis by analysis*) and he easily became angry and frustrated when things went wrong.

I pulled him back from the brink of insanity through the use of concentration exercises, as I have described before and, after a short time, he began to enjoy the game again.

We devised a simple programme of "thoughts" to help him round the course and, particularly, to occupy his mind during the shot. It helped him enormously. It may help you too.

On the opening holes the "game plan" is to swing the club freely using the "Club Head Awareness technique.

The club head is going to pass through two specific points in the swing. The first will be when it arrives at the very end of the back swing and the second when it makes contact with the ball. Your FOCUS is simply to be aware of the club arriving at those two points. There is no success or failure for this exercise – only a greater or lesser degree of awareness. You will be surprised how good the shot is the more aware you are of the club head during your free swing.

The fact is that the club, during a swing, is rarely where it "should be" but it is always where it is! Being "with" the club head works wonderfully!

After a few holes your concentration/awareness of the club head will have produced its rewards and you will have settled down with a degree of confidence. Your "thinking" may well change to PLANNING WHERE TO PLACE THE SHOT and you may reach that lovely state when you simply play the shots without any thoughts at all.

Of course, golf being a game of mistakes, things will go wrong occasionally (accidents happen) when suddenly you will press the shot or hurry the swing or, even, have a sudden doubt about the outcome. On these occasions your conscious mind is intruding, once again (as it does), blocking your natural brainwaves that produce your "perfect, natural swing".

Having made your mistake, you can learn from the body language – the physical experience.

You must not worry about the "one-off" poor shot but if it repeats it cannot be ignored.

Instead of trying to put right what you think went wrong, your focus for the next shot will be simply to find out *at what precise moment during THIS swing you feel the tightness, or the snatch come in.*

Let Go totally and focus all of your attention to this one thing only. Do not be disappointed if you no longer feel that tightness (*or whatever*) because in all probability you will have been so absorbed in finding that moment as you swing the club freely that the source of the anxiety, the fear of failing, that caused the tightness in the first place, will have been eliminated.

In other words, the more absorbed you become in one thing, the less worried you will be about another. Remember that the "conscious mind" is the culprit so get it into "awareness mode".

This is by far the best way I know of coping with disasters and sudden "loss of form" during a round.

Too often I hear of players who became so angry with themselves at making a bad shot, or score, at one hole that it has affected them for several holes thereafter.

Your bad shots are history (*accidents, really*) and can never be altered or put right – they happened and you are simply left with another shot to play – and another opportunity to recover.

Through relating your swing to "feel" and listening to your body language you can dump your emotions and play outside of your *conscious mind* IMMEDIATELY – and recover.

During a round, of course, you play some "super" shots which are miles off target – but don't start adjusting everything because of a "one off" shot. This will make your mind uncomfortable again and fill you with doubts. Learn from the *pattern of shots* before adjusting your set up during a round.

So, to really enjoy your game walk away from the doubts, fears and all things negative.

- *Absorb yourself in "what is,"* (*not in what should be*). What happened last time is history and can never be changed. The future hasn't happened yet so worrying about it has no logic. Calm your mind by concentrating on club head awareness during your free swing.

- *Listen to your body language* and discover at what precise moment on your next swing you feel the tension come in.
- *Plan for WHERE you are going to send the ball* and play one shot and one hole at a time.

COUNTING YOUR SCORE HALF WAY ROUND LEADS TO FAILURE. It places pressure on you to keep doing well – or to try harder to recover. Count the score at the end.

- *Learn from the pattern of shots* and adjust your set up or grip.
- *LOOK FORWARD TO EVERY SHOT and* FEEL LIKE A GOOD PLAYER

Only Two Things Can Go Wrong

October 1984

Yes, there are really only TWO things that can go wrong in contacting the ball, and that must come as a tremendous relief to most of you.

It all rather depends, of course, on your point of view and if you are one of the legions who are still trying to keep that *head down* and the *left arm straight*, and are still battling to *swing the club by numbers as* per the text books, then you could, justifiably, argue that there are hundreds of things that can, and do, go wrong when swinging the club this way.

I am quite certain that everyone who reads these pages – and others in this magazine – will have enjoyed the fullness of the T.V. coverage of this year's Open Championship – The Open – and marvelled at the skills of the greatest players in the world.

Do you imagine they were all reminding themselves of what they *should be doing* as they swung the club? No! Not even those who spent hours on the practice ground *after* each round that they played.

It might well be argued that they had, in hitting thousands of balls, grooved their swing to something which they could rely on, and trust, and that the swing they ended up with only became *NATURAL* after hundreds of lonely hours on the practice ground.

It would be presumptuous of me to say that this was not so because I haven't spoken to, or conducted "in depth interviews" with, the likes of Nicklaus, Crenshaw, Faldo, Trevino, Zoeller and Ballesteros – nor, even, have I met them (yet!) but I do know this – that all of these golfing superstars swing the club in a "different way" and yet all of them swing it "similarly".

All of them swing the club around the right ear, and then around the left.

All of them keep their head reasonably still – NEVER DOWN – allowing it rotate a little as the shoulders turn.

All of them allow the body to be "accommodated" during the swing as the lower half slightly resists the top half in the backswing; and allow all hell to be let loose in the downswing!

All of them give the impression that the forward swing is an *automatic reaction* to what occurred in the backswing.

So, what is NATURAL and what is GROOVED?

I, personally, don't think there is any difference EXCEPT that these "gladiators" mentioned above have hit so many balls that they know their own swing and trust it – in spite of the obvious fact that their swing is *unique* to them.

They may well have focused on keeping their knees flexed during the backswing to create greater resistance and "torque" and they may have practiced for hours to find out where their hands are in relation to the club head. They may well have hit balls until sunset to instil the feeling of the arms swinging independently of the body.

Does one swing the club naturally until it is grooved, or groove the swing until it is natural?

This, of course, is a question that can be argued until the early hours – there can never be a clear-cut answer ... well, maybe, there is!!

What I do know is that when I ask my clients (all handicap categories) who attend my Golf Schools to *feel heavy at address* and *soft in the hands and shoulders* they can swing the arms independently of the body ANYWHERE they like COMFORTABLY; they consistently hit the ball further and straighter than when they try to apply all the "correct" mechanical moves that have been recommended by the golf swing analysts.

So perhaps we have to get things into context.

Tournament professionals can be likened to Formula One racing cars whose engines must be finely tuned for optimum performance on race day. The car and the driver act and react as one – in perfect harmony. So, too, the swing of the golfer must be balanced for power and accuracy for the tournament, where feel and finesse must also play a vital role.

We lesser mortals, on the other hand, should liken ourselves to a Ford/Nissan (they and others are the "most reliable of motor cars") simply to get us safely from A to B without breaking down.

So, too, our own golf swing must be one we can rely on, and since we trust the many physical movements which carry us through each day without conscious thought, we should trust our natural swing and learn from the shape of the shot.

All of this brings me back to my opening remark: there are only two things that can go wrong in contacting the ball,

1. *The club face can be delivered to the ball either "open", "square" or "closed" to the swing path.*
2. *The swing path can be either to the "left of", "square to" or "to the right of" the ball-to-target line at impact.*

In earlier articles and in virtually every golf book ever written a good golf grip has been illustrated and explained with sound, logical, reasons for adopting such a grip. Indeed, such a grip should be used in an ideal world – but since we don't live in an ideal world, we must adapt ourselves to what works for us as individuals.

The hands do control the club face. However, unless the hands are able to return the face of the club SQUARE TO THE TARGET at impact, we must alter something in the grip which will enable us to do this. There is absolutely nothing wrong in doing this – if it produces the right result.

Do remember that the tour pro hits thousands of balls each week and his golfing muscles are finely tuned.

Those of you who play once or twice a week, or even three times, will have hit a hundred or two (full shots), depending – the remainder being Chips and Putts. Hardly the stuff to generate a "good hands/club face relationship"!

So, if your ball drifts to the right towards the end of its flight repeatedly, the face was "open" to the swing path. MOVE BOTH HANDS TO THE RIGHT on the handle.

The player whose ball spins toward the left towards the end of its flight is delivering the face CLOSED to its swing path, and should, therefore, MOVE BOTH HANDS TO THE LEFT on the handle.

To develop a good hands/club face relationship *both palms should face each other when gripping the club.*

Each and every one of us is a complete individual. We are, every single one of us UNIQUE and, if for various reasons, we are limited through age, physique, lack of mobility/flexibility or, even time, we must adopt a set up and/or grip which enables us to deliver that club face square to the target at impact.

Remember, the manner in which you swing the club is of no consequence so long as your swing repeats and you have control of the ball.

Here we have to make up our minds. Is it a HIT or is it a SWING?

Once again we have to look at those *Gods of the Links*, the tournament pros, who appear to swing the club with varying degrees of fluency, dispatching the ball enormous distances through the air.

Rest assured that to every single one of them their SWING (*like the Formula One engine*) generates enormous power to the point where, through impact, the club face is travelling in excess of 120m.p.h. – but the SWING came first.

Most handicap golfers crave two things: consistency and distance. Give me *control of the ball* any day – and this comes from a good set up and grip! You will achieve greater distance, naturally, if *the shoulders are soft, the base is firm and heavy* and the *arms are swung freely*.

I was talking to the wife of an acquaintance the other day and suggested that, once she had set herself up at address, she should swing the club as though it didn't matter where the ball went. She looked at me "wide-eyed and horrified" and that was that!

Later in the day after her round she expressed her amazement at how much further the ball went with so little effort. I'm not sure whether she was grateful to me or not because a whole new problem of club selection presented itself as she kept going through the greens!!

Forgetting about distance keeps the shoulders soft and relaxed, allowing the arms to swing freely.

Forgetting about … enable you to *focus on se… club face swing through the b…* the target. This will give you more accuracy, consistency, control of the ball … and distance!

I have said it for years (and others have said it too) – the ball is "in the way of" the club head that passes through it at speed.

The ball is "collected" by the club face *"en passant"*!

Concentrate on your set up and let the spin of the ball tell you about your grip.

distance will being the to

1984

⌐the ⸺ are the name of day's world.

① ②

1. The Pulled Hook. The swing path is to the left of the target line, and the clubface is closed to that swing path. To rectify the problem, check the ball position in relation to your stance - you will probably have to bring it back a little. Also check that you are looking over your left shoulder to the target and not around it. If the ball spins to the left move both hands to the left.

2. The Slice. The swing path is to the left of the target and the clubface is open to that swing path. To solve the problem, move the ball back in the stance so that the shoulders automatically align themselves more to the target. Feel soft in the shoulders and move both hands to the right on the grip. Sling clubhead through the ball.

I suppose the word, to most of us, conjures pictures in our mind of satellites beaming T.V. pictures "live" from the other side of the world; of "fibre" cables handling hundreds of telephone calls at a time; of computers getting smaller in size and bigger in output; the silicon chip and all that "stuff".

Perhaps we have become so used to, and reliant on, all of these things that the true art of communicating verbally is dying.

We tend not to explain ourselves clearly enough; misunderstandings arise and, suddenly, everyone finds themselves "up all sorts of creeks without the proverbial paddle".

Feeding information is one thing but how it is interpreted is another.

Memories at this moment come flooding back to me of halcyon days at Prep School as packs of boy cubs charged around collecting badges and stars to, proudly, attach to our jumpers.

"Relaying a message" featured prominently, as I recall, whereby the first cub was given a message (of great import!) to deliver to another. First, though, he had to climb a tree, dig a hole and run round the cricket field before relaying the message to the second cub. The second cub would run off to ring a bell, knock on matron's door and find a feather before relaying the message on to the next … and so on. No doubt our female counterparts did much the same.

You can almost see and feel the industry of it all as these little mites ran around frantically rehearsing and repeating "their charge". You can "live" the disappointment when it was revealed that *"The castle is surrounded by a moat"* came back as *"The parcel was eaten by a goat"* ... and we all scratched our heads and blamed each other, wondering where we went wrong!!!

Every day, somewhere, the spoken word is misinterpreted or misunderstood. Somebody, some- where, "picks up the wrong end of the stick"; someone else gets frustrated because no one understands his or her point of view.

It all seems rather crazy in this world of sophisticated communication. The power of the spoken word is losing its edge ... or is it only happening to me?

I received a lovely letter the other day from a reader who enjoyed my articles. Not only did he think the information was good but the style in which it was written had a relaxing effect on him and was helping his game.

Since he had followed my series of magazine articles from the beginning he wondered when I was going to explain what was meant by THE SHAPE OF THE SHOT. I THOUGHT THAT I HAD – MANY TIMES!!!

On looking back through earlier copies I certainly mentioned the phrase often enough, but at no time did I give a full explanation of what is meant by it. Yet here I was in my little world assuming that I had got the message across and everybody knew exactly what it was that I was talking about.

I wonder how many of us fall into this trap in business and in our daily lives.

Last month we took a general look at the two things that can go wrong when contacting the ball, and this month we should look at how we can relate the flight of the ball in the air to the information we feed into our address position.

Until we understand fully what the ball is telling us and relate this information to our set up, we shall continue to blame our swing, to contort and contrive and to dream up all manner of compensatory moves to keep the ball in play.

As I have mentioned many times, a FREE SWING OF THE ARMS is fundamental. Trust this swing and blame, instead, your poor position at address for those irritating errant shots.

For those of you who still "heave with the shoulders", "pick the club up", "hoist it" or "flick the wrists" then nothing in the world will improve your "shape of shot" until you swing those arms freely and independently of the body ... and pay attention to your initial "input" at address.

Feel HEAVY at address and SOFT in the shoulders – this will enable you to swing the arms around a still(ish) head and "secure platform". Thereafter you truly can learn from the flight of the ball.

We now know that most of our mistakes are in our address position – before the swing begins and that, thereafter, there are only two things that can go wrong:

1. *The swing path, at impact, can be to the right, or left of the target line*, and
2. *The club face can be "open" or "closed" to the swing path at impact.*

Let us take a look at some of those shots where the swing path is to the *left* of the target line

THE SLICE

- *The swing path is to the left and the club face is open to that path.*

This seems to be the handicap golfer's nightmare but, actually, there is nothing with such a ball flight if it is kept under control. "Slicers" will know that they tend to slice with their middle to long irons and woods; that their favourite club is a six, seven or eight iron and that they generally miss the green on the left

with their lofted clubs. They also know they tend to lack distance.

This is because the longer, less lofted, clubs impart *side spin* on the ball whereas the shorter, more lofted, ones impart *back spin*.

The common denominator is that the swing path is to the left of the target at impact.

You may well have taken care to align the club face to the target at address.

You may well have swung the club freely with the arms (less likely) BUT THE ARMS CAN ONLY SWING IN WHICHEVER DIRECTION THE SHOULDERS ARE ALIGNED AT ADDRESS.

The ball is too far forward (to the left) in the stance causing the shoulder line to be aimed to the left.

- MOVE THE BALL BACK IN THE STANCE a little. That will allow the shoulder line to be aimed, naturally, parallel with the ball-to-target line.
- Feel SOFT in the shoulders so that the arms CAN swing freely and you'll notice a new swing path as the ball will set off to the target.

So, we have made a major alteration WITHOUT CHANGING YOUR SWING.

Since the "slicer" has seldom been in the habit of delivering the face of the club "square to its swing path" (it is almost always *open* to it) he will probably do the same with the new, improved one also. So, now that we know it is the HANDS THAT CONTROL THE CLUB FACE, we should MOVE BOTH HANDS TO THE RIGHT ON THE HANDLE (palms "facing each other").

Set Up for a better swing path and "sling" the club head through it. COURAGE, MON BRAVE! Don't be frightened of finding out what happens. TRUST your natural swing and LET GO of your inhibitions. How else can you learn what this adjustment to your set up can do to the "shape of the shot"?

THE PULL

- *The swing path is to the left of the target with the club face "square" to that path.*

This shot is very nearly a very good golf shot but, unfortunately, there is little pleasure in hitting the ball well, but off line to the left.

Once again, the "aim of the swing" is to the *left* because the BALL IS TOO FAR TO THE LEFT AT ADDRESS. MOVE IT BACK a little to "re-align" the shoulders and stance parallel with the ball-to-target line. Since the ball flies straight to the path of the swing there is no need to adjust the grip.

THE PULLED-HOOK

- *The swing path is to the left of the target line but the club face is "closed" to that path.*

This is a "crippling" golf shot which sends the ball into the deepest rough - starting off left and spinning further to the left. Horrid!!

Now we know that to change the path of the swing we must move the ball BACK IN THE STANCE.

We also know that the hands control the club face – which, in this instance is "closed" to the path of swing. We must MOVE BOTH HANDS TO THE LEFT ON THE HANDLE (palms "facing each other").

To repeat (again, sorry!), the only five factors which make up the address position are:

- Grip
- Aim
- Stance
- Ball position relative to the stance, and,
- Posture

... and all of these things influence the direction of your FREE SWING and the alignment of the club face at impact.

LEARN FROM THE SHAPE OF YOUR SHOT & ADJUST YOUR SET UP OR GRIP.

TRUST & LET GO!

Get Out of Your Own Way

December 1984

I was beginning to think I was losing the war with one of my pupils recently.

Concentration on breaking the wrists during the takeaway will open the clubface to the swing path. This results in a loss of both distance and accuracy.

She had definitely won the early battles and my resources were running dangerously low as I had almost run out of ways to stop her from "trying so hard" to hit the ball "properly".

I was almost out of ammunition when something I said (*must have been a stray shell!*) caused her to get off the surface of trying, whereupon she hit the ball rather well a few times in succession.

I considered this minor skirmish to be a victory – well never having won even a minor skirmish in this war to date I was going to, wasn't I?

At least it gave me time to redeploy, to study my strategy for the counter-attack that would inevitably follow.

This lovely lady had come to a golf school as a complete novice and planned, quite rightly, to follow this up with a few sessions privately. The school would set her on her way and the private sessions would accelerate her debut on the course. That was the plan.

There should be no independent hand action during the takeaway. Allow the arms to swing freely to the side and let the shoulders turn softly in sympathy.

I knew that war had been declared the morning I gave a lecture to the school on concentration. While the others sat on the edge of their chairs wanting to hear more, she was giving me that GLAZED look! It wasn't a glazed look that said that is "poppycock" ... I can tell THAT sort of look! ... It was a look that said "That is alright for the rest of them but it won't work for me until I can play". THAT sort of look!

I got on to the subject of "Getting out of one's own way" (*Chasing achievements gets in the way of your progress*) by allowing the swing to be what it wanted to be ... well, once you have "set it up" you HAVE to let it go if only to find out how good it really *could* be ... and "feeling it" and "seeing it" in a totally non-judgmental atmosphere.

The more I got into the subject, the more the rest of them sat on the edge of their chairs –and the more GLAZED the look got on this lovely lady's face. The others, of course, had never listened to, or heard, anything like this before.

Finally, the lecture over, we went to the practice ground to "discover" how CONCENTRATION GAMES could accelerate our progress, and increase our levels of potential ... all, that is except "Glazed Eyes" who came out to TRY TO HIT THE BALL!

"War it shall be" I said to myself, and, always being one to go straight into the deep end, I went to her first.

Can you imagine the scene?

I knew what she was going to do (*Try Hard*) and she knew what I was going to do (*Try to STOP her from trying hard*).

Like two gun-slingers in a Randolph Scott Western movie we stalked each other.

Ol' Glazed Eyes and I unblinkingly anticipated each other's move as we circled the ball.

Finally, she settled herself over the ball. I eased myself into position in front of her – SLOWLY, for she was a MEAN CRITTER!!

Then she "looked" at me. She tossed her head as if to say "O:K, buddy, go for it, any time you like."

I asked her to swing the club FREELY with the arms, ANY WAY SHE LIKED, and ANYWHERE IT WANTED TO GO. She was not to attempt to do anything she thought she OUGHT to do but to let it come out any way at all. All I wanted her to do was to "BE" with the club head all through the swing. I wanted her to BE AWARE of the club head arriving at the end of the back swing, and of the milli-second it made contact with the ball - to OBSERVE it... nothing else.

She gave me that LOOK again!

"O.K." she said.

The shot was AWFUL – and I mean BAD!

Keeping my sense of humour, I enquired "Well, were you with the club head?" "I don't know" she said "I was trying to turn the shoulders!"

The swing was slow, deliberate and contrived. (*First skirmish to her, I thought*).

"Fine" I said, "Let's go for it again. I really don't mind where the ball goes, or even if you miss it – and I don't want you to mind either. Just be with the club head arriving at the two points in the swing."

"Right" she said in a tone that suggested she MIGHT play the game.

The swing was slightly less pedantic (*but still too slow and contrived*) and the result was, again, terrible – another "scuttler" to the right.

"Well"? I enquired somewhat gingerly.

"I tried to make my swing longer". (*Another skirmish to her, I thought*).

After five minutes I was covered in bruises. I had an arm in a sling and a leg on a crutch. I was being BLASTED out of existence … and always THAT LOOK! OI' GLAZED EYES was making a mess of me. To say that we were not on the same wavelength might be the biggest UNDERSTATEMENT of this year!!

After further abortive attempts to help her "get out of her own way" I limped away SEETHING at my seeming inability to release her from her "bondage" of TRYING TO BE GOOD, and DOING IT PROPERLY.

As I walked down the line of the others, I found a new bounce in my step as I listened to the pleasant chatter of pupils making their "discoveries".

I discarded the CRUTCH when "Charlie" DREW a drive for the very first time, being seemingly surprised that he could find no tension in his swing. I threw away the SLING when "Jim" hit a bad shot and didn't lose his temper. "I was with the club head all the way to the end of the back swing then lost it about two feet before it arrived on the ball."

"That's O.K." I said "let's find out where you lose it this time. Observe."

The next shot was terrific.

"Wow, I was with that one ALL the way" he said ignoring the extra distance with draw he had just imparted on the ball.

Feeling more revived I returned to the end of the line where my lady friend was working away diligently.

A too early wrist break on the takeaway was opening the face of the club to the swing path and her shots, therefore, lacked distance and went off to the right.

"Help" she said.

"There is no independent hand action on the takeaway" I said. "Allow the arms to swing freely to the side of you and let the shoulders turn softly in sympathy. There will come a point towards the end of the back swing when the wrists will hinge naturally – IF you let them. Let them hinge and you will then be in a position to swish the club head through the ball."

We stood for a moment chatting which helped her to settle down again.

"When you make a cup of tea, add milk and sugar, stir it all together and take a sip, do you give a lot of conscious thought to the movements you make?" I asked.

"Well, I think about how much sugar to put in and being careful not to spill it" she replied.

"Sure", I said "but do you THINK ABOUT HOW TO DO IT?"

"Of course not", she answered "that's automatic."

"You mean that your movements come out automatically?"

"Yes, I suppose so", she said "because I've never really thought about it."

"Then," I suggested, "let the movements of your swing be just as automatic. Let them be NATURAL and COMFORTABLE, without thinking about them."

"I can't because I have to hit the ball," was the reply.

"YOU don't have to hit the ball," I countered "the CLUB FACE will do that."

I went on to explain that, fundamentally, the golf swing is nothing more than a free swing of the arms. The only "rules" were to "set up" well, to give the swing a "platform" by feeling "heavy". Feeling "soft" in the shoulders would give her this physical sensation. The body merely turns twice giving energy to the free swing of the arms.

Instead of TRYING TO SWING PROPERLY and HIT THE BALL she should, first of all, experience what a free swing feels like. Without placing any importance on how the shot came out she should, for the moment, simply enjoy the experience of a free swing.

She returned to playing a few shots but, now, she was no longer frowning. The anxious look had disappeared as she swung the club freely from side to side.

"Make room for the swing," I encouraged her, "by letting your body turn in sympathy – on both sides.

Now she really was "swinging freely" and enjoying this new experience.

I asked her to notice the precise moment that the club head arrived at the end of the back swing and also the precise moment of contact with the ball as she turned to the finish.

Suddenly she "got off the surface," no longer trying to succeed. Her swing came out quite differently to all her previous attempts.

Gone was the deliberate "straight back slowly for the first 12 inches followed by the early wrist-cock" (*yes, she HAD read a book or two!*). Gone, too, was her exaggerated "tilt of the shoulders" and "narrow arc". Furthermore, her swing was "balanced" – from start to finish.

"I enjoyed that", she said, smiling.

"I ENJOYED THAT," I said smiling also "How did you do that?"

"I don't know", she replied, "It just happened automatically. "All I was thinking about was on seeing the club head pass through the ball."

I sensed the smell of victory for the very first time in the whole of this campaign.

I suggested to her that if this was all she was thinking about then, surely, her swing must have been NATURAL.

She played some more shots and every one of them was a huge improvement on all the others that had gone before.

We talked some more and I repeated some of my remarks about concentration during the lecture earlier. I reminded her that "chasing achievements gets in the way of progress", that "trying hard fails" and that the only way she would reach new levels of potential would be by trusting her natural swing, by giving it good information in terms of grip, aim and stance at the start – and by getting ABSORBED IN WHAT IS – in a totally non-judgmental atmosphere.

She looked at me and her eyes were alive. The GLAZED LOOK had gone.

I retired, battle-weary and scarred but I had won a major victory – one that could shorten the war!!

Curing the Push and Hook

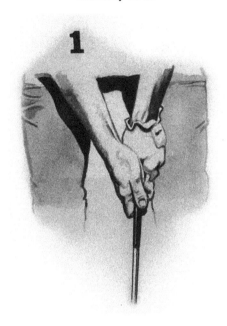

1. The hands control the clubface. Whatever the hands do the clubface will do. In taking a grip of the club it is imperative that both palms face each other.

"Life is like that" I thought to myself when I saw the quite UNDELIBERATE mistake which features prominently in a previous article I wrote.

A magnificent graphic shows the club face "square to the swing path" which is going to the "left" of the target line (a "Pull"), while the "*caption*" describes the club face as being CLOSED to that path creating a "Pulled Hook". Wrong! The "pulled

hook" is, indeed, the result of the face "closed" to the path that goes to the left. Clear?

We are all allowed to make mistakes, and there is nothing wrong in that, but the irony of this "boob" was that the subject of the article was COMMUNICATION and how that at some point along the way we get our lines crossed ...? (*What was that about "Moats and Goats"??!!*).

2. Wherever you aim it you will send it. So make sure your shoulders, hips and feet are aimed directly at the target.

Now, undaunted and still in confident mood, we are going "go for it again" and look at those shots

87

which start off to the RIGHT of the target.

The ball can do only these things once struck:

It can set off:

- To the right of the target
- Straight to the target, or
- To the left of the target

In addition, the ball can spin in the air:

- To the right
- Go straight
- To the left

3. The swing is restrictive if the stance is too wide. As a general rule your feet should be about shoulder width apart.

Now all those of you who are still looking for those "secret moves," which will produce a particular "Shape of Shot," will forgive me if I remind them (*again*) that a "free swing of the club with the arms" will produce a reaction on the ball, and THAT REACTION will be dependent on how one stands around the club and ball at address.

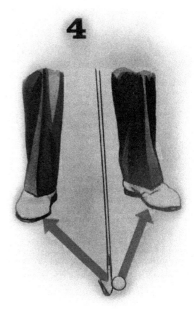

4. It will be no coincidence that the ball will find itself in the middle of your stance for the left foot for the less lofted ones, WHEN everything is squarely line up.

It is absolutely true to say that the "shape of one's free SWING" will be slightly different in setting the ball off to the "left" of the target, than it would when setting it off to the "right" – but that, too, is a result of one's initial address position.

Until you completely understand that ONLY FIVE factors influence the reaction of club face meeting the ball – and that THESE alone matter – you will continue to dash up blind alleys and get lost in the maze of "bunkum and dogma" that is strangling your game.

Sorry to be "boring" but I have to repeat this again (and again!) – the direction and flight (spin) of the ball are conditioned by:

- Grip
- Aim
- Stance
- Ball position in stance, and
- Posture

THESE THINGS ALONE will determine the outcome – given a "free swing of the arms", "soft shoulders" and a feeling of "heaviness".

To "rectify mistakes" (*that occur often, even with a "free" swing*) one has to be "One's own DETECTIVE" – because the "clues" will be lying there, most likely, somewhere in the address.

You already know the other possibility – the "physical feel" of the swing - but that is for later.

So, what does the "PUSH" tell us?

The ball has set off to the right of the target but it has no side-spin on it – it flies straight. It doesn't take a Sherlock Holmes to discover that the club face was "square to its swing path," but that the path was travelling in the direction to the right of the target … therefore the AIM of the swing was poor (to the right). "Simple, Dear Watson – check the set up routine and body alignment."

The "HOOK" tells a similar story in that the ball sets off to the right but with a subtle difference. The ball spins in the air in a counter-clockwise direction causing it to swerve to the left in flight.

Once again one must check the "aim and ball position in the stance" (*ball too far back?*). One might also move both hands to the "left" on the handle.

5. *Stand a comfortable distance from the ball. Stand tall - but get those hips out of the way. Feel balanced, poised … and heavy.*

The "PUSHED FADE" is yet another irritating shot. You know the one – the ball sets off to the right of the target and spins in the air to the right also.

Once again one should check the aim of the swing (*body alignment*) and ball position (*too far back?*). One should also check and, maybe, adjust the grip by moving both hands to the "right" on the handle.

Remember the old adage "If the ball "bends to the right" move BOTH HANDS TO THE RIGHT. If the ball "bends to the left" MOVE BOTH HANDS TO THE LEFT". Simple!!

NOTHING IS COMPLICATED!! The "solutions" are SIMPLE.

"Learn From The Shape of Your Shot – Adjust Your Set Up and Grip – Trust & Let Go" has been my "mantra" for years.

IGNORE AT YOUR PERIL WHAT THE SHAPE OF YOUR SHOT IS TELLING YOU. Golf will never give you pleasure if you do.

Keep It Simple and Avoid Confusions

February 1985

A pupil of mine who had made good progress during a course of lessons came to me the other day in a state of confusion.

I knew something was on his mind from the way he was swinging the club that morning. The "elasticity" and "fluidity" which he had been developing nicely over the weeks before was missing and I could sense that he was trying to find whatever it was he was looking for – so much so that, for much of the time, he was unaware of what I was saying to him.

Being an extremely self-critical person, the atmosphere reached a dangerously "electric" level. The exasperation he felt with every poor shot filled the air – rather like the "buzzing" of overhead cables in the rain – and I felt he was going to explode in a fit of fury unless I did something – fast!

Experience has taught me, in such situations, to completely shift the focus of the exercise, and to do something entirely different for a while until things had "settled down," so I asked him to play a few gentle Pitch shots to the green.

He enjoyed this part of the game and we had fun playing shots from a few feet to about 50 yards.

The "buzzing of the cables" ceased and the voltage in the atmosphere decreased the more he relaxed and "unwound". The anger he felt some moments before disappeared as he, lazily, lobbed another ball over the bunker to settle close to the pin.

I wasn't "doing" anything by way of instructing him. We simply chatted idly as he played those little shots.

After several minutes I sensed he was about to come out with whatever it was that was on his mind.

91

"You know that I am entirely in your hands and have faith in everything that you say."

"I'm pleased", I replied. "... And, you know, when I let things happen the way you suggest I make some wonderful shots!"

"Yes", I said, "and not only do you hit the ball better and further when you let your swing be natural – it LOOKS better too."

"Well," he continued, "I do understand now the importance of having a good grip, and I see how essential it is to have a good set up and posture around the club and ball, and when I get rid of the tension in my shoulders, particularly starting the downswing, I'm very pleased with the results."

"Good," I said "now tell me what's on your mind!"

"You've never told me what I should be doing with my LEGS."

Oh Lord! I thought to myself – WHO has got to him – WHAT has he read?

"Read anything recently?" I asked, slightly tongue-in-cheek and resisting a smile.

"Well, YES", he replied "and I jolly well wish I hadn't because now I'm very confused; and I certainly haven't hit a decent wood shot or middle iron since."

He went on to say that he had read in a popular Sunday newspaper how Seve Ballesteros starts the downswing with his knees, and now he was confused because I had been encouraging him to experience the "softness" in the SHOULDERS so that the ARMS could "swing" the club freely through the ball. I had, indeed, been teaching him to swing the club with the arms and to "find the ball with his hands" – but I had never mentioned anything about the legs.

I tossed a ball to him and asked him to throw it underarm onto the green.

"What started the forward movement?" I enquired.

He thought about it for a bit, then said that he didn't know. He had simply thought about throwing the ball onto the green.

I asked him to throw another but, this time, to pay attention to what he felt did start the forward movement of the throw.

After several throws he said that the initial movement was a mixture of his knees sliding and the hips-midriff turning.

"O.K.", I replied, "Now throw the ball making a conscious effort to slide the knees and clear the left side out of the way".

The result was disastrous! He almost forgot to let go of the ball – and the "knees slide and turn" were made in a grossly exaggerated fashion. In "thinking "about this he had totally lost all his NATURAL COORDINATION.

I handed him his No.5 iron and invited him to swing the club freely for a moment or two. I reminded him that the only purpose of the swing was to deliver the club face square to the target at impact and his FOCUS was to "see" the face pass through the ball. Having "set up" well I encouraged him to swing the club as though it really didn't matter where the ball went.

"So, swing the club naturally the way YOU would like to swing it – not the way you THINK you should do it – and learn about your grip and address position, and the "feel" of the swing, from the flight of the ball in the air" I said.

He swung the club freely again and that "elasticity" returned. The shot was good and he smiled as the ball flew over the distance marker post.

"Swing it freely again", I said, "and LET the shoulders feel loose."

Another fine shot came out.

"What triggered off the down swing?" I asked. "Play another shot and find out – from what you FEEL. Your FOCUS will remain the same, to dispatch the ball to the target, but this time pay attention to what you FEEL PHYSICALLY moves first in the downswing."

Once again he relaxed as his "curiosity" was aroused and an "interested" look came into his face. Another VERY good shot came out

although it didn't appear to excite him all that much.

"Well, I felt the knees sliding a little as the weight transferred with the body turning, but I have absolutely no idea "precisely" in which order it all happened."

"What else did you feel?"

He played several more shots (all good) paying attention to the physical experience of the swing itself. The whole atmosphere was "comfortable" and "calm". With every shot he discovered all manner of "feelings". He no longer JUDGED anything, being now in a most relaxed mental and physical state.

He was "aware" of the arms swinging freely … the club head swishing through the ball … the shoulders loose and soft … and on several shots he told me excitedly that he really WAS aware of the club head at the precise moment it made contact with the ball.

The rest of the session was very enjoyable (for both of us) because not only was he playing good golf shots, but he discovered that HIS NATURAL SWING produced the very same movements which he had read about in his Sunday paper. He learnt also that the more he TRUSTED, the more distance and accuracy he achieved.

He was relieved and happy again that all was well; and resolved never to read instructional articles again!

"Good Heavens," I said "don't do that. We'll all go out of business." But I did warn him to be careful about how he interpreted what he read, reminding him that communications in oral or written form can produce different interpretations and reactions in different people.

The main message which comes out of this is that ANY PHYSICAL MOVEMENT INDUCED BY CONSCIOUS THOUGHT IS INEFFICIENT.

All of us are UNIQUE. We are "one offs" and if we set out modelling our golf swing on somebody else it would be completely artificial – no longer OURS. While it might work for a while it will not last and will break down at the slightest hint of pressure.

Your swing can only be "natural" if you do NOT "think about it". Your "natural swing" will be influenced by "your" age, physical make-up and flexibility. It is who you are!

Given a good Set Up and, given a "relaxed mind and body" throughout, your "natural swing" will become even more efficient when YOU LOSE YOUR FEAR of making a mistake.

We all, on occasions, have a "bad day at the office" – things happen. Don't "invite" these days to you by misinterpreting what you read.

Besides, who really cares if you have a bad day?

Your dog will still wag its tail when you return home at the end of the day!

Listen to Your Body Language

March 1985

We have to get it into perspective before the whole thing leaps away from us, and before we go chasing up blind alleys again.

The position of the right knees should never move during the backswing. All too often the handicap golfer "wobbles" on his base, allowing the knee to slide to the right or straighten

So, let us look at the ONE thing that ALL the really good players do.

I fear that I am in danger of falling into the trap of "teaching positions and contortions" and so I will hastily add that YOU will end up doing the same thing NATURALLY once you establish a good posture and set up at address – and have initiated the "one-piece" takeaway (*as described previously*).

Remember, the shape of your swing will be very much influenced by your own physical make-up. The taller person will naturally swing the club on a slightly more upright plane than the shorter one – but in every case of the high calibre player whether he be Ballesteros or Langer, Pate or Stadler, THE POSITION OF THE RIGHT KNEE NEVER MOVES from the beginning of the takeaway to the end of the back swing.

The higher handicap player often, through an incorrect takeaway, either "wobbles" on his base allowing the right knee to slide to the right, or through a poor pivoting action of the hip (*normally because of a poor posture at address*) allows the right leg to straighten at the end of the back swing.

"Now, look here", I hear you say "this is getting TECHNICAL. You are back to "mechanics," and if I have all this to think about how can my swing be "natural?"

Well, I do understand your worries, but again would hasten to add that far from wanting to teach you "movements by numbers" you CAN swing similarly to those great players (*depending on your own physical make-up with all its strengths and weaknesses*) by LISTENING TO YOUR OWN BODY LANGUAGE, relating your swing to FEEL or, to put it another way, by being "aware" of THE PHYSICAL EXPERIENCE OF THE SWING ITSELF.

In many cases, the pupils who come to me for help are too emotionally involved in simply hitting the ball better, and are oblivious to the physical feelings, or experiences, of the swing movement.

Generally, with every unsatisfactory shot, they move away from this essential feedback, becoming more and more emotional about their failure to succeed.

Like any good teacher I have a quick eye and ready knowledge of what caused the ball to react off the club face and several earlier articles have explained some of these causes and effects.

In most cases a simple alteration to the grip or other set up adjustment provides the solution but, although going away feeling better (*emotionally and physically*), the player may not be aware of the difference those adjustments made to the shape of the swing. And why should they, when the swing feels natural again and the results much improved?

One thing that I absolutely HATED when I was younger was to be told "DON'T DO ..." this or that. Clients don't like it either. This "command" produces even more conscious thought, doubt and uncertainty – and fears about "getting it wrong again".

On the first morning of a School I chatted to the group, as I always do, making the point that if we were all to get something out of the course I needed their "open minds".

All the "stuff" they had been taught previously; all the "gimmicks" they had picked up along the way; all their preconceived opinions and ideas of what they *should* be doing should be "put in a box" and left in the corner of the room for the duration of our time together. I allowed them to put their own names on their box, however!

I was quick to point out that I was not suggesting I alone knew how to teach, nor that what they had been taught previously was wrong; but that unless I had their completely open mind they would be less likely to make the progress they were seeking.

I witnessed the look of horror on some of their faces as I suggested they "dump" everything – but they relaxed a little when I told them that, at the end, they could pick up their box and take it home with them IF THEY STILL WANTED IT!!

"Tightness", as we know, is the killer of a free and liberated swing. We also know that it comes from doubt about how you think it looks (*to others*) and, of course, about the outcome.

In many cases the tension in the shoulders restricts a free turn of the upper body that causes the right leg to straighten in the back swing.

One of the great "consistencies" of all good players, regardless of individual "style," is that the right knee maintains its "flex" from the address right through to the end of the back swing – and this comes from the feeling of HEAVINESS. It is not complicated – it is a simple matter of FEELING IT … of being AWARE of it during the movement.

It does not require "conscious thought" to make you try to do it. You cannot *"try to do"* a FEELING!

Are your hands "tight" on the handle? FEEL how they are. Do they start off "light," then tighten their hold at some stage during the swing? FIND OUT. BE AWARE of the moment that they do.

There is no point in telling yourself "Don't tighten the hands," or "Don't straighten the right leg in the backswing," because, assuredly, they will tighten and/or it will straighten all the more.

The ONLY way to solve "physical problems" in the swing is to pay attention to "how it feels" – to increase your awareness of WHAT IS … not on what "should be".

By "listening to your body language" and by finding out at what precise moment during the action you "feel" the sensation kick in, the problem miraculously, disappears.

The CONSCIOUS MIND is the culprit. It knows nothing about "how to do" anything. It is a bully, it is judgmental and sees, always, the negatives. In truth it really wants to help you but, simply, does not know how.

What it is very good at is, when so directed, OBSERVING – being AWARE of WHAT IS.

If one feels physical tension during the swing it is because the conscious mind has inserted emotional stress through its warnings of probable disasters that lie in wait.

But if, on the next shot, you ask it to search for the precise moment the tension kicks in – what part of the swing, what part of the body – it will search for it. Remember, it wants to help. It will be calm as it searches. It will be so attentive and, being so focused, the SUBCONCIOUS MIND – the ultimate achiever – comes out to play. All tightness disappears.

Having been introduced to this "Mind Management Process" the clients really were able to improve their golf – every single one.

So, be attentive to what you feel – to the physical experience of the swing itself.

By the end of the School and having said our farewells it was not surprising that there were many "boxes" that were left in the corner of the room!!

97

Ten Ways to Improve Your Consistency

May 1986

CONSISTENCY! There is absolutely no doubt that if we prayed earnestly to the Great Golf God for the one thing above all others that we desired in giving us more pleasure, it would be CONSISTENCY. If only that god could grant us our wish!

Most people when asking me to improve their consistency are really asking me to help them hit their BEST SHOTS – ALL OF THE TIME and, clearly, this cannot be possible. Golf is a game of mistakes, remember?

The consistent golfer must surely be the golfer whose bad shots do not detract from making a good score.

Even if it were possible to be "granted this wish" you can easily imagine how the 28 handicap player will quickly become disenchanted with his or her best shots when compared with a much more experienced golfer. Furthermore, the whole meaning of the word takes on a new "hue" the moment this 28 handicap player hits the longest drive of his or her life that landed in the centre of the fairway. Their "consistency" from then on will be measured against those rare shots that come out only now and again.

Whether you are a struggling tournament pro seeking to save ONE shot a round so as to "make the weekend," or whether you are merely trying to play to your handicap you must look at this whole subject realistically – and in different ways.

Whatever your level of experience, to contact the ball "more consistently" means that you simply wish to reduce the margin between YOUR BEST and WORST golf shots. Nothing more!

Quite obviously, if, as a club golfer, you have ambitions to improve you will be working with your pro and putting in some practice, as there is no "given right to progress". We EARN the "right" through our own hard work – in all things in life.

One can play more consistently without hitting the ball like a pro and, depending on your handicap, all that is required is a clarity of mind when playing on the course.

In my experience I find that many people out there, in spite of seeking a more stable performance, will stand to the ball and "hit and hope". These people have neither a clear picture in their minds as to "what works" and "what doesn't," nor do they have a clear picture of what they want the ball to do.

Never attempt a shot that is beyond your capabilities.

Instead, give each shot a target and forget about hitting the green on a long par 4, if your handicap tells you that you are not expected to reach it in two.

Many others may have practiced hard but, on the golf course, still do not "trust" themselves or their swings. Others, again, through mental and physical fatigue find their game going through "peaks & troughs" – good holes interspersed by poor ones.

Perhaps we can recognize ourselves in these illustrations but we CAN all play better golf more consistently on the golf course if we simply "keep our head on our shoulders" and have a clear and realistic view of things.

KNOW YOUR LIMITATIONS

Never attempt a shot that is beyond your present capability. There is nothing more true than that "more gamblers LOSE than WIN".

If you are developing a positive visualization of a successful shot BE REALISTIC in what you can achieve.

KEEP IN THE PRESENT TENSE

We know that the game is made up of "nearly", "not quite" and "almost" golf shots and that, now and again, we play the "perfect shot".

We must remember that the future hasn't happened yet and what happened in the past is history. And we can do nothing about either.

It is perfectly possible that the next shot will be successful so "Set Up" perfectly, "link your mind to the TARGET", "take the risk" (of making a mistake) and "swing all the way to the finish". Be aware of your rhythm – or of the club head passing through the ball. TRUST … & LET GO.

LET YOUR MIND REST BETWEEN SHOTS

When Walter Hagen talked of "smelling the flowers along the way" I am sure many people misinterpreted this classic remark.

There is no doubt that he did enjoy fast cars and parties but this great player (who did not have a great swing) had the ability to "switch off" BETWEEN SHOTS. He noticed the clouds in the sky, the leaves rustling in the trees and the people and things around him. He gave his brain a rest until it was time to play another shot, but, once over the ball, he would get right back to planning, visualizing and applying himself to the immediate matter in hand.

BE PATIENT

All of us can become irritated by our unsuccessful shots and/or our bad luck but only the patient golfers are able to play themselves out of these slumps.

Try to keep to your plan and to your procedures because, in any event and even when making some mistakes, someone has to beat YOUR score to win – and who knows what kind of horrors the rest of the field are enduring, or will encounter.

I used to loathe playing in the wind but have since learnt to be patient knowing that the same wind is blowing on the heads of all the other guys too and that they, also, would be making their mistakes.

UNDER PRESSURE PLAY THE SHOT YOU KNOW

Sometimes, things don't always go right when we are out there – no matter how much we have practiced.

Some people respond well to the challenge of making a good recovery shot or of "grinding it out" when not swinging the club well. For others the "confidence crisis" (lack of it) is a statement of loss of self-belief.

In most cases it is best to play the clubs you have most trust in, and play the hole "another way" – regardless of if they may not be the appropriate ones for the hole. Two 7-irons on the fairway are better than a 3-wood (hit into the rough) and a poor recovery shot – or two!!

PLAN WHERE – NOT HOW

"See" only "a good shot".

If there is a doubt in your mind about the shot you are about to play being successful, CHANGE YOUR PLAN (and your club) – until you "CAN see a good one".

DON'T COUNT YOUR SCORE UNTIL THE END

Play one shot and one hole at a time – and avoid the "All I have to do" syndrome.

Too often golfers, playing well, get ahead of themselves ... counting their scores too soon before the end. Result ... Bogey, Bogey, Double-Bogey: no prize, no speech ... no cigar!!

For myself I still cannot decide what gives me more pleasure – to swing the club well and make a good score, or, to swing the club poorly and "grind out" a score?

PLAY THE COURSE, NEVER THE MAN

In match-play competition one is often paired with a lower handicap golfer who is evidently "more experienced," and who will hit fewer shots and strike the ball better, etc.

If you, however, play the course USING YOUR HANDICAP and within YOUR LIMITATIONS he is going to have to play very well indeed to win – the handicap system being what it is.

THE POWER OF CONCENTRATION

It does NOT mean to think about what one is doing!

It means to ABSORB oneself in what is going on at the time IN A NON-JUDGMENTAL ATMOSPHERE.

Focus on WHAT IS. BE AWARE of the rhythm, fluidity, the club head passing through the ball ... ANYTHING else. (See "Mind Control").

RELAXED AWARENESS promotes a "carefree" swing, keeps one off the "emotional surface about having to succeed or avoid failing" – and leads to better results.

VISUALIZATION

Never under-estimate its power!

In life, as in golf, whatever one "sees" on one's mental movie-screen one gets, and whatever one "thinks" one gets, too (See GOALS).

The choice is yours.

"I knew I was going to do that" is the famous cry as the ball flies into the water, the bunker or the trees.

It is just as possible to "see" a good shot – the ball landing on the fairway or the green.

It is only a matter of TRAINING THE BRAIN. This takes practice, too, however!

Finally, KEEP IN THERE. You can't be dead if you are still breathing!!

Always complete your score at the end of the round.

The truth is that "YOU ARE A WINNER" – even though your name is at the foot of the stack – and you will always beat the "nil-returners" (the "whiners") who gave up because the going got too tough.

Check Your Footwork for More Consistency

Circa 1985-87

A young tournament pro contacted me a little while back to say that he was in a muddle and needed some advice.

He had already sought the help of several other respected teachers, all of whom had told him he wasn't swinging his arms enough in the downswing. But no matter how hard he tried he was unable to stop hitting the "pushed-fade", that crippling shot that starts off to the right of the target and bends further to the right. It was, as he said, creating havoc with his scores and confidence.

Having read some of my articles he knew me to believe that the arms must swing independently of the body and hoped I could give him the solution and release him from his torment.

As we were talking on the phone I had no way of knowing what exactly was going wrong with his swing, but there were definite clues and so, like every good detective, I began at the beginning.

"Clearly, for the ball to behave in this fashion," I said "the club must be travelling in that direction at the moment of impact and, for the ball to "bend" further to the right means that the face of the club is facing to the right of this swing path. There are two possibilities," I went on, "as to how this mistake is occurring but only one factor common to each of these possibilities".

I went on to tell him that the arms could be swinging down faster than the body turns out of the way and, since the arms have nowhere to go, they will continue to swing the club to the right on an "inside-to-out" swing path. But this would surely result in the ball going straight to the right, or even to "hook".

I was pretty confident in my diagnoses that the body was not turning to the left through impact.

"Alternatively," I said "your hips are sliding laterally towards the target to such an extent that the club head is being left behind. I suspect that your feet are too wide apart at the address which is causing this reaction. If you were to stand with the feet closer together you would find that the body would be able to turn more easily and naturally creating more club head speed through the ball".

"Well", he said "no one has ever told me THAT before but I will give it a try".

"Start off hitting a few balls with your feet together", I suggested, "gradually drawing them apart until they reach shoulder-width – but no wider – and call me back in a few days".

A week later he called again to tell me that the "pushed-fade" had gone completely and, now that his feet were less far apart, he was finding it so easy to turn his body to the left in the forward swing, enabling the "centrifugal forces" to fuel and energize the free swing of the arms and club through and beyond impact.

He was delighted to make much more solid contact with the ball again.

Naturally I was pleased for him, and pleased with myself also, because I know only too well what it feels like to endure these bad spells. I also felt thankful that I do not play golf for a living!!

We agreed that he should come over to work with me in person as he had other questions on his mind; things that were confusing him.

When he arrived a few weeks later we were filming his new address position and "new" swing … and he was swinging the club very well indeed, making great golf shots, and evidently enjoying himself.

Every now and then he would come out with a question that had been preying on his mind. You will appreciate that when pros get together they usually exchange ideas about their techniques and other things they have 'picked up' along the way.

"To play consistent good golf you must understand that the 'ball is your instructor'. It tells you all you need to know about the alignment of the face at impact, the path of the swing through impact and the plane of the swing that makes the ball fly high or low" I said. "Everything depends on how and what you Set Up because this determines what happens next".

"I'd rather you didn't discuss techniques with your friends", I told him "because everyone is different both physically and, even, mentally. They have their own "ideas" on how things should be done".

"Are my arms swinging down fast enough now"? he asked me.

"What is the ball telling you and how does it feel"? I replied.

"I just feel as though I'm doing nothing and yet the ball is coming out of the sweet spot every single time … and I haven't felt this good for a long time".

I went on to explain to him that 90% of golfers feel they have to 'hit the ball' with great force using the strongest muscles of their shoulders and back, and it is for this reason that I encourage a free swing of the arms independently of the body to those amateur players.

"You, however, are now at 'scholarship level '. At your level you now know that distance and effort are unrelated but you should be aware, by now, of the role played by the feet and legs in the golf swing". I went on to explain the feet and legs either get the body into position to do something, or, to get the body out of the way for something else to happen.

We spent the next minutes in virtual silence save for the lovely sound of the crisp contact and the 'sizzle' as the ball flew through the air.

"Widen your stance once more," I asked him. The "pushed-fade" returned immediately!

"Point made – and taken" he said with a grin.

Setting Your Goals Too High

A Gentleman attended a School last summer with the purpose of making radical improvements to his game.

Being fit and forty (plus a year or two) he saw this as an opportunity to shave strokes off his handicap which was in the middle teens.

By lunchtime on the first day he had already made progress and although our work had been confined to the Short Game, he was enthusiastic about his achievements in flighting the ball over the greenside bunkers without taking his customary deep divots. Very quickly he experienced a new feeling of balance, rhythm and "freedom" during the movement.

As we progressed after lunch into the middle irons his smile was broad and pleasure genuine, and his own good feelings were spilling over into the others in the School – such is the power of group-learning.

Naturally I was feeling good too as I moved from pupil to pupil, happy in the knowledge that I had 'got through to them' so early in the course and I was looking forward to our 'review session' at the end of the day when we would talk about our 'discoveries'.

Alas! By the time I had reached the end of the line and had returned to my enthusiastic friend there was a silence – an atmosphere; and the vibes I was picking up were not good!!

"Tch! Another dreadful shot" he exclaimed. He was not amused and no longer smiling. The perspiration was dripping from his brow as he snatched another ball from the bucket and launched in to another assault.

It was, I decided, time to stop for the day as I was hearing some of the others complaining about their bad shots. This often happens when we stay out there too long. Fatigue and mental boredom kick in.

When I appeared, there was a "hush" in the room. People were draped over their chairs with chins on their chests, and there was a definite "sense of humour failure" throughout.

I flung myself into the 'lion's den' by asking if anyone had learnt anything from the day's practice – something which worked and which they had remembered. SILENCE!

"What about you"? I asked my friend, who had lost, not only his sense of humour, but also his will to live!

"I feel like I've got worse instead of better", he remarked. I have NEVER hit the ball so badly as I did during that last hour. I'm really depressed".

This remark sparked off other comments from the tired group and, it must be admitted, that if I had not encountered this sort of reaction at the end of a first day before I could have had a problem, and, probably, have felt depressed myself. NO ONE was smiling!!

"What happened this morning with your Short Game?" I asked hoping to rekindle those memories of enjoyment and achievement, "and again, just after lunch, when you were thrilled to see the improvement in your middle irons?"

"Well, I admit that for a while I did OK," he conceded, if a little grudgingly, "but I wasn't able to sustain it, and I just feel that this new swing you have given me just doesn't work all the time".

I reminded him that I hadn't given him a "new swing" at all but that HE had discovered what it was to swing the club freely for the very first time, in a state of balance. Furthermore, I reminded him of his own words earlier in the day when he felt, for the very first time, his hands 'delivering' the club face square to the target at impact

instead of his normal habit of 'heaving' the club down onto the ball.

His mood was such that he didn't want to be convinced of anything because he was tired and unhappy with himself so I agreed to leave it for another day and suggested we retire to the bar before cleaning up for dinner.

The next morning I reminded everyone of the dangers of hitting too many balls and of how easy it was to drift out of a "learning and rehearsing" phase into one of aimlessly thrashing golf balls.

"Don't get lost in your own square yard", I urged. "I want more noise, more chatter, more moving around and much more listening to me as I deal with the others".

I wanted them to take it easy today and reminded them that the real learning came, not from the number of balls they hit, but from a complete clarity of mind. "When the body and the mind get tired there is no learning at all", I said.

By lunchtime I had a really happy group on my hands. There WAS a lot of chatter and laughter. There WAS a lot of coming and going as clients came and listened awhile before returning to their station and, even, my friend had re-located his enthusiasm for life ... and for golf.

"I've always been concerned about the 'one-piece takeaway'", he said, "and my worries became greater when you told me to swing my arms freely, anywhere they want to go naturally in the backswing. But I've discovered that when my shoulders are really loose at address, and when I can feel them to be relaxed it seems that my arms do swing freely, but that the shoulders also turn at the same pace as the arms swing the club away from the ball".

He demonstrated the point and hit a series of very good golf shots.

"I really CAN feel the arms swing the club into the back of the ball. Usually I feel my shoulders tensing up at the start of the downswing", he admitted.

"GREAT", I said, "Take a seat. Have a rest … and ABSORB what you have discovered. Clarity of mind stays with you only for as long as you are fresh. Don't hit too many balls and tire yourself out, no matter how much you are enjoying yourself".

His enjoyment was spilling over to the others who were all making good progress and I was really looking forward to our 'review' session at the end of the day knowing that THIS TIME it would be a happier occasion.

Well, it takes a good hour to go down the line dealing with each pupil with all the individual and diverse problems and by the time I returned my friend, once again, was quiet. I watched the perspiration flow from his brow and, once again, I was amazed at the speed with which he was 'belting' each ball.

"Clarity of mind" I enquired?

"THAT hasn't worked for the past hour" he replied. "Nothing has. How can it suddenly desert you like this"? The impatience in his voice was coming over crystal clear. "I'm worse than ever again".

By the time we returned to the video room for tea my friend was questioning whether to take up bowls but, undeterred, I, once again, invited the others to come out with their own discoveries and, this time, there was a better reaction.

One person was delighted that for the first time in his golfing life he hit the ball out of the middle of the club face without thinking about 'method and technique'. His only swing thought was to keep the shoulders relaxed throughout the whole swing.

Another realized the importance of a good posture at address and discovered how much better his shots were when he held his head HIGH – not DOWN as is so often recommended.

Overall, the mood was positive and there seemed to be an 'energy' in the air … except, that is, for my sullen friend who remained quiet and pensive throughout the proceedings.

"I discovered that I can't play golf", he announced grimly, "and probably never will be able to play it. I just don't understand how it is that I come out with some great shots and then, for no apparent reason, and thinking I am doing exactly the same thing, I revert to being worse than before I started".

His statement fell upon the ears of the others and, in a sense, dampened the atmosphere.

"Have you discovered ANYTHING about your good shots today"? I asked, remembering clearly his announcements earlier in the afternoon.

"No. Nothing" he replied as though to confirm his current mood.

I reminded him of his morning's work and the pleasure he derived and, eventually, like a dentist pulling teeth, managed to extract from him some positive comments. It was evident that he was terribly depressed at his inconsistency, but still didn't admit to having hit too many balls and got mentally and physically tired. His attitude was that if he could do it once he should be able to do it all of the time.

We were getting nowhere in our conversation but I wasn't going to let go, feeling that I really HAD to improve his "attitude" as well as his game.

"How GOOD do YOU THINK YOU SHOULD BE"? I asked him, "because it is quite evident to me that your idea of 'good' is quite unrealistic"?

"I don't know" he replied "but I should be better than I am".

"But you have already told me that you played a large number of shots that were beyond your wildest expectations" I said forcibly.

"But I can't do it every time" he came back, equally as forcibly.

Changing the subject, I asked him what he did for a living. "I'm a doctor", he replied.

"When did you first decide that you wanted to be a doctor"? I asked

"Oh, I suppose when I was doing 'O' Levels" he replied. "Alright", I said "Then what? University? ... and I expect you did at least a three-year course there"?

"Yes" he answered, wondering about the reasoning for this line of questioning.

"... and after university I expect you served an internship in a hospital? How many years? Three?

"Yes"

"... and then, I imagine, you found a position as a junior partner in a practice somewhere".

"Exactly that"

"Well, I don't know but after four or six years you either moved on feeling that you were ready to start your own practice, or you were invited to join your existing team as an equal partner in the firm"? And for how long have you been a senior partner in your firm"?

"About fifteen years" he said.

"Are you a GOOD doctor"? I asked.

"No, not really" he said. I am sure he is a really good doctor but you have to remember the mood he is in.

"So" I said "after all the years of studying, the hours each day, the exams, the self-denial and all this time of concentrated effort to your subject amounting to 29 years you consider yourself NOT REALLY VERY GOOD"?

"If it's taken all this time and effort to become 'mediocre,' HOW DARE YOU EXPECT SO MUCH OF YOURSELF IN A SUBJECT TO WHICH YOU DEVOTE ABOUT 6 HOURS EACH WEEK"?

By this time I was being quite forceful myself. The others in the room who had been obliged to listen to this cross-examination in silence suddenly came to life again and 'buzzed' with a new excitement having realized that they, too, had put too high an expectation level on their performances. Several admitted that their enjoyment of the game had been marred in this way.

My friend sat quietly for a while and I wondered what was going to happen next, for I had been pretty rough on him!

"I DID hit some really good shots today and, on reflection, I now know why. Let's see what tomorrow brings".

There Is No Point in Kidding Yourself

Circa 1985-87

Attitude is the all-important key to better performance.

"Hitting the ball badly, or hitting it well, is equally OK"

When I say this to my clients on the practice ground or in the lecture room, I must admit I get a lot of reaction. Well, at least I know they are still awake and listening!!!

Some gasp in astonishment that I should make such an absurd statement, some are derisory, whilst others will give me that "glazed look" that says they know I have finally snapped but won't let on.

I still believe it to be true, however.

Of course, no one enjoys making poor golf shots and, more particularly, if they repeat them frequently, because they can affect our attitude.

Consider this. How we "see" an event approaching us affects the way we respond to it, and the way we respond to it affects the way we "see" ourselves. This, in turn, affects the way we "see" other new events approaching us. No one can disagree with that!!

We really ought to recognize that EVERYONE IS A GOOD GOLFER – IN SOMEONE ELSE'S EYES and if we did, we would all enjoy ourselves more when playing the game.

The novice will look at the 25 handicapper and call that person a 'good player' whilst the 25 handicapper will look at the 15 handicapper and call that person a 'good player' – who will, in turn, look at the pro and say that's a 'good player' ... and who is to tell that the pro will look at Ballesteros and call HIM a 'good player'. You see now, what I mean.

All that we need to do is to 'act and behave' like the good player we are AT OUR LEVLEL IN THE GAME.

Too many things get in the way of this logical approach. Surface things ... emotional things take us away from the reality of where we are in the game, and this affects our attitude as to how we approach another golf shot or event.

Things like THE FEAR of FAILING. If we have failed on a few previous shots those 'memories' lie uppermost in our minds, and we are likely to approach the next shot in a doubtful and uncertain manner.

Failing can bruise our egos and diminish our confidence – or it can teach us something.

For as long as we allow our ego to dominate our moods, we won't learn anything from what the shot is telling us; and neither will we get the 'feedback' from the physical feeling of the swing which resulted in the poor result.

Since the manner in which the ball flies through the air is only a REACTION caused by;

- The club face alignment at impact
- The path on which it was travelling through impact, and
- The plane
  … and, since these are influenced by;
- The grip
- Aim
- Stance
- Ball position in relation to the stance, and
- Posture

… we will learn nothing from those messages the shape of the shot is giving to us, being as we are, on the emotional surface of simply trying not to fail. All the solutions lie in the above but our negative attitude prevents us from applying them.

"Expectations" can affect our attitude. If our own expectations are too high or, if others' expectations of us are high, we reach the point where we lose sight of REALITY, forgetting where we are in the game.

As I have said "ALL golfers are 'good players' in someone else's eye" – at their various level of experience – and it is right and good that we wish to improve, but we must be clear about what is realistically possible AT OUR STAGE IN THE GAME.

An 18 handicap player is considered to be a really good golfer by all those with a higher one, but is not 'expected', nor should expect him or herself, to Par most of the holes. Why, then, does this player attempt to hit the greens 'in regulation' like the pros when "his or her par" on a 72 Par course is 90? The fact is that this Net Par 72 is a very good score.

Of course, this 18 handicap player can "realistically" expect to achieve a gross par on some holes; short Par 3, short Par 4 and, should he or she accomplish that, then those 'put him in credit' that offset other more costly mistakes that might lie in wait later.

Some people tell me that this is being 'negative' and that one should attempt to 'stretch the boundaries' by striving to 'play to par,' but my reply is always the same – "The quickest and surest way of lowering one's scores and handicap IS TO USE IT". Do what you know you can do and select targets you know you can reach. This is called REALISM.

Such an attitude would invoke a calmer approach to the shot in hand and produce a freer swing that will result in a better shot – and a lower score!

It always fascinates me to listen to the various comments as clients chastise and criticize themselves over their performance when, in fact, for most of the time they were playing well at their level in the game.

Bob, a delightful septuagenarian who just wanted 'ten more yards' (!) hit a wonderful 5-wood which 'faded' into a greenside bunker. He turned away in disgust muttering that he had wanted to 'draw' the ball. I had to quickly remind him that, with his handicap on this long Par 4 hole, he had no right to be there in two shots at all! A bunker shot and two putts would give him a net par.

When he arrived at the bunker I could see that he was determined to make a Par and, once again, I had to jump in to save him from himself.

"Hang on", I said, "I know you would PREFER to play a superb bunker shot and I don't doubt that you can, but it doesn't matter where the ball lands on the green because, with two putts, you will walk off with a net Par. Don't attach any special importance to this shot".

A bunker shot and an 8ft Putt later he walked off with a huge smile on his face and his first gross Par of the day.

"What about that terrible 5 Wood shot that ended up in the bunker that you complained about"? I asked him. "Actually, I was quite pleased with it. I've never hit one so far in years – and it didn't matter that it was with 'fade' rather than 'draw', did it"?

"Of course not", I said, "it was a very good shot that was not expected to go so far".

Another pupil had had so many bad experiences with his woods that, not only did he not use them any longer, but the inhibitions he felt were affecting his performance with the irons as well.

His swing was ragged and the atmosphere as he stood over the ball was, to say the least, ELECTRIC!

By the mid-afternoon of the second day of the school his swing was coming out more fluidly and he was hitting some very fine shots, so I went over to him and suggested that now he should use his woods, since there was little to be learnt from always playing his favourite clubs.

He snatched his 3 Wood from his bag, as though to take it by surprise, but, once again, the atmosphere became charged as his muscles tensed up.

"Hey", I cried, "where's the freedom gone? Loosen up"!

"I can't", he replied, "I have a WOOD in my hands"!

"I don't care where the ball goes but I want you to swing the club anywhere that feels comfortable and focus all your attention on the EXPERIENCE of rhythm, balance and elasticity that you found with your irons".

It took several swings and lots of encouragement before he finally "let go" of his inhibitions … and then he hit a CORKER!

"Too high", he said.

"Ugh"? I spluttered, dumbfounded.

"The ball flew too high"

"It was a SUPER shot", I said, "at least 170yds ON THE FAIRWAY"

He played another of about the same distance which flew a little lower.

"Tch", he said.

"Something is in your teeth"? I enquired.

"I hit it a bit 'thin' and it didn't come out of the sweet-spot but, at least, it went a good distance"

After several more shots and lots of complaints I had to remind him that he was now hitting his woods for the first time in years and that, by his own admission, he was getting far better results than ever before, so why was he still so dissatisfied with himself when they weren't 'perfect'.

I suggested that he was a perfectionist of chronic proportions and that until he looked at, and accepted things, in a more realistic manner, he would get little pleasure from the game.

A day or two later we were all playing golf and I teamed up with my friend for the final three holes.

"I'm only taking my wood because YOU are here" he chuckled.

"Fine, let's go"

He hit a great drive and followed this up with a 4 Wood to the front of the green.

"Well done", I said, feeling really pleased for him.

"A bit LOW", he said - but I could tell by the look in his eyes he was pulling my leg!

The messages in all of this are clear. If we want to improve our performance, we have to train our brain.

- Failing simply provides an opportunity to LEARN
- USE your handicap – and watch it tumble.
- Be REALISTIC about your limitations and expectations.

Discard What Doesn't Work

I was asked if I would give a lesson on playing side-hill lies.

Little did my pupil realize that I wasn't going to TEACH her at all but that SHE was going to show ME how to play these shots!

We went to the practice ground, to a spot where the ball was above the level of her stance. She had a 5 Wood in her hands.

Apparently on a certain hole at her club she always 'fluffed' her shot from this kind of lie and, since she felt that the shot called for this club, she wanted to practice with that.

The ground sloping towards her worried her because she had many unhappy memories of "topping" the ball from this situation in the past.

"What shall I do"? she enquired.

I suggested that ANYTHING would do to begin with because by simple process of elimination we would discard all the things which didn't work. I encouraged her to play a shot or two.

The first shot she played she "topped" – but she had predicted that she would!

"What causes a 'topped?'" shot" I asked.

"It's because the right shoulder heaves the club on the downswing," she replied.

It was quite a reasonable reply I thought to myself, before offering that A STEEP ANGLE OF ATTACK across the target line (i.e. to the left) was the prime cause of this irritating shot.

She set herself up for another and looked at me with hope in her eyes that I would give her the 'magic move'.

"We discovered something that doesn't work," I said and so there seems little point in continuing with THAT method".

"What do you mean"? she asked.

"Well, a steep angle of attack doesn't work when the ball is above the level of your stance".

"How do I swing it flatter?"

"I don't know", I said "but swing it, using your instincts, anywhere you FEEL better able to return the club face to the ball".

I thought I would save a little time by suggesting she stood a little taller and a little closer to the ball, and, to hold the club slightly further down the handle.

She swung the club – a nice swing on a much shallower plane. She missed the ball completely! Her look suggested that I had done something wrong!

"We have discovered something else." I ventured.

"What", she countered "That a flatter swing misses the ball completely?"

"Yes" I replied "WHEN THE BALL POSITION IS SO FAR FORWARD IN YOUR STANCE".

"But I thought that one was supposed to have the ball nearer the left foot when playing a fairway wood" she said with just the slightest bit of frustration because, over the weeks, she had been working really hard on improving her address procedure.

"The ball is ABOVE the level of your stance", I reminded her "and if the normal set up doesn't work in this situation we must do something else".

She admitted that the flatter plane of swing did FEEL better in this instance so I gave her permission to move the ball back to the middle of her stance – just to see what would happen.

She allowed her instincts to draw the arms and club away from the ball on a plane which would easily enable her to deliver it back again. This time the shot was good. In fact, the shot was tremendous.

"I'm really disappointed with that," she said as she watched the ball start off directly to the target then veer violently to the left. "Why? Didn't it feel good?" I enquired.

"Oh yes, but it missed the target on the left".

"Fine," I said "we've just discovered something else."

"What?" she asked.

"The ball will react this way IF YOU AIM YOUR SWING DIRECTLY AT THE TARGET".

"I think I will aim this one to the right, then" she said.

The smile of satisfaction which followed the next shot was a delight – as delightful as the shot that started off to the right before drawing back on to the green.

I will say this to my clients until the very end of time, LEARN FROM THE SHAPE OF YOUR SHOT, ADJUST YOUR SET UP OR GRIP TRUST … & LET GO.

All too often I see people on the practice ground 'perfecting their mistakes'!

"Why continue with this method," I say to them "you've proved to yourself beyond all shadow of doubt that it doesn't work? If you continue with it you will become the complete authority on this poor shot, having rehearsed it for so long".

Learn what the flight of the ball is telling you and adjust ANYTHING to suit the situation. LEARN FROM THE EXPERIENCE.

My pupil discovered that, through a logical process of elimination, she could play good golf shots when the ball was above the level of her stance.

She didn't learn 'how' because I had told her what to do. She had learnt from her EXPERIENCE of what went before. Everything that 'failed' was discarded. Everything that worked better was a DISCOVERY, and was 'banked' into her subconscious for use on another occasion.

If I had simply told my pupil what to do and how to do it, she would, quite automatically, try to execute the shot well and remember all that I had told her. She might well have become inhibited in case she 'got it wrong'.

But by dealing with her problem in an atmosphere of calm logic, where everything was a 'discovery' she will remember the experience forever and re-live it on future occasions, now that she knows what does and doesn't work.

"Can I play some shots where the ball is below the level of my stance?"

"Of course you can and very well, I imagine". I replied.

"What shall I do?"

"ANYTHING – swing the arms freely and let's see what happens", I said.

She adopted her usual stance for a 5 Wood … and 'topped' the ball.

"I couldn't get the club head to the foot of the ball", she said.

"Fine, so what are you going to do about it? We've discovered that, in this situation, a normal stance doesn't work".

"Bend my knees more?" she offered hopefully.

"If that's what you want to do let's see if it works".

She swung the club freely again making good contact with the ball but lost her balance and pulled the ball to the left.

"What causes a 'pulled shot'? The swing path is to the left of the target at impact with the club face square to that path. What might cause that?" I asked her.

She thought for a moment and then suggested, quite rightly, that the ball might have been sitting too far to the left in her stance.

She brought the ball back in her stance and made another swing. I had reminded her that she could swing the club away from the ball in whatever plane would enable her to return it to the ball again. The swing came out freely once again but, this time, with a little steeper backswing and her balance was good – but the ball, although starting off straight, faded to the right.

"Another 'discovery"? I asked.

"Yes", she said "and now I'm going to aim the next shot to the left". The next shot was Brilliant!!

Natural learning can only come from experiencing things in a NON-JUDGMENTAL atmosphere. In other words, there are times when we have to experiment with some things.

I was discussing the subject with a low handicap player from The Emerald Isles who had been to one of my golf schools and who had made his own 'discoveries', and since it seems that everybody in Ireland knows each other, he was able to tell me of his conversation with one of Eire's greatest golfing sons who felt that, since it had taken him 25 years of lonesome hours on the practice ground before he got 'good', then this 'natural stuff' must be nonsense.

This poses the question – do you groove a swing until it feels natural or swing the club naturally (within the boundaries that will make it efficient) until it is grooved?

Whichever way you look at it there is nothing more certain than the fact that before anyone achieves 'greatness and success' in anything he must first have experienced failure.

The world's greatest golfers spent hours on the practice ground discovering what did, or didn't, work. They will have worked on the fundamentals of Set Up and Posture, or whatever, UNTIL they came across the thing that produced the desired result. Then, they 'banked' the experience and practiced it until they could reproduce it in the thick of the tournament when under great pressure, having the confidence to do so.

Let us take a look at some of the things that DON'T work so that we can discard them from our game.

FAULTY GRIP. Most golfers think they have the perfect grip. Most golfers are WRONG! The club sits in the 'roots' of the fingers of the right hand so that there is a conflict between where the palm of the hand and the face of the club are looking.

There should be no independent hand action on the takeaway.

Liken the movement to a door on its hinges. The shoulders, arms, hands and club, or in other words the whole unit, move together round a stable base.

WHAT DOES WORK? Grip the club in the 'crook' of the middle two fingers (right hand) – rather like 'shaking hands' with someone. By opening the fingers, you will find that the palm of the hand and the face of the club will be looking in the same direction.

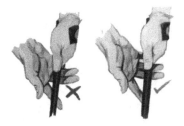

The wrong and right ways to grip the club in the right hand. The illustration on the left shows the wrong method. Here the club is being gripped in the "roots" of the fingers. The correct method illustrated on the right, shows the club being gripped in the "crooks" of the middle two fingers of the right hand.

EARLY WRIST-BREAK IN BACKSWING. This is not recommended, as independent hand-action early in the takeaway can lead to the club face 'opening' or 'closing' to its swing path.

WHAT DOES WORK? A smooth one-piece takeaway works better. The arms and club go 'together' - ANYWHERE NATURALLY - whilst the shoulders that are LOOSE turn easily.

The Perfect Grip. The club is held in the middle joints of the two middle fingers of the right hand - not the roots.

FEET SET IN 'CONCRETE'. Many people, in going for that 'heavy feeling' and 'stable base', lock up the feet and legs to the point where all mobility is lost.

WHAT DOES WORK? A Feeling of RELAXED HEAVINESS works best and it promotes the 'springiness' in the feet and legs.

The main thing is that one's swing must be natural and comfortable because this is the 'perfect swing' for YOU.

The Set Up Routine is fundamental and critical as to what happens next. This must never be taken for granted.

Playing off sloping lies is just a matter of Set Up. One must not be frightened of 'experimenting' with this until one discovers what works best.

I think it was Edison who said, when searching for the secret that would give the world light, "Each failure I have brings me closer to success. Each failure is a method to discard because it doesn't work".

He was light – sorry, RIGHT.

Conclusion

Leap forward almost 40 years.

The world has changed and now our lives are dominated by mobile phones and the internet.

So much has changed in this time that one wonders how one coped with fax, phone calls and photo-copying in years gone by! Personally, I never was able to use a fax machine; I no longer have a telephone land-line at home and I am never without my mobile phone these days!!

Some things, however, have not changed - nor ever will they for as long as golf is played.

- THE BALL-FLIGHT LAWS (the cause and effect of club face meeting ball), and the

- PSYCHOLOGY required if one truly wants to be an achiever and enjoy playing better golf.

One without the other does not work.

One must truly understand the first before one can apply the second.

The third thing to understand is that "style does not matter". All of us are wonderfully unique. It was never intended that we be 'cloned' with any other person or golfer.

I confess to often being repetitive, but it is vital to establishing the clarity of mind so essential to your progress.

John Jacobs once told me that given his time again, he would have paid much more attention to the psychology in the game and I, likewise, wished, as I wrote these articles as a much younger man, that I had paid more attention to VISUALISATION and the TARGET.

I have broached the subject here in these pages but it wasn't until I had read a whole lot more on the subject that I 'majored' on both as my career developed.

Experience, they say, is the best teacher and these comments reflect this perfectly.

I hope, however, that you have enjoyed these selected articles and have picked up some ideas that will improve your play and enjoyment of the game. If you have picked up on the importance of learning from the shape of the shot and the 'input' you give to your set up, you are well on your way to playing better golf without consciously changing your swing.

I am not going to wish you "luck" – you don't need that any more – but I do wish you "good bounces", when playing, and many "single putts"!

Most of all I wish you HAPPY GOLF. Even when, sometimes, we have that "bad day at the office" just remember how privileged we are (healthy enough and wealthy enough) to be out there. Think about others. Think about that!!

Have FUN. TRUST & LET GO

Lightning Source UK Ltd.
Milton Keynes UK
UKHW020657040121
376381UK00005B/77